ESSENTIAL HANDBOOK FOR KGB AGENTS

English version is published
by the Industrial Information Index,
Suite, 3, Cavendish Court, 11-15 Wigmore Street,
London W1.

Comments in italic interposed with the text are from the English version publishers. The photographs obtained from different sources have also been added by the publishers.

ESSENTIAL HANDBOOK FOR KGB AGENTS

PUBLISHED BY
THE USSR COMMITTEE FOR STATE SECURITY
MOSCOW

Top: Felix Edmundovich DZERZHINSKY (1877-1926), the founder of Cheka in Tsarist prison.
Bottom: As head of Cheka together with Iosif Vissarionovich Stalin.

FOREWORD
FOR THE ENGLISH VERSION

The KGB have, for the past 74 years, been justifiably feared as an organisation whose responsibilities were almost as diverse as their methods of acquiring information. This ideological police-force were in charge of intelligence as well as security at state borders, nuclear installations, weapons programming and other similarly sensitive tasks. In the event that they had need to enforce their will, they were able to draw upon a garrison of over 200,000 specially trained troops, and an army of several million informers.

The initials KGB stand for *Komitet Gosudarstvennoy Bezopasnosti*, or Committee for State Security.

The Committee's creation was suggested by Lenin and realised by the Polish revolutionary Felix Dzerzhinsky (1877-1926) in 1917 under the name of VChK (*Vserossiyskaya Chrezvychaynaya Komissiya*, or All-Russian Extraordinary Commission), better known as Cheka.

Several unsuccessful attempts to improve the public image of the organisation were made, involving a change of name. It was first changed on 6th February 1922 to GPU (*Gosudarstvennoye Politicheskoye Upravleniye*, or State Political Department), then on 23rd November 1923 to OGPU (*Obyedinyonnoye GPU*, or Amalgamated State Political Department). Other changes were yet to come.

The Committee's first chief was Felix Edmundovich Dzerzhinsky, one of the few in that position to die a natural death in 1926. His job was taken over by Vyacheslav Rudolfovich Menzhinsky (1874-1934), who for twelve years followed the guidelines laid out by Lenin and Dzerzhinsky, jailing and exterminating everybody suspected of disagreeing with Party policies.

As Menzhinsky come to know too much about Stalin's crimes, in 1934 he was replaced by Genrikh Yagoda (1891-1938). Once again, on 10th July 1934 the name of OGPU was changed, this time to NKVD (*Narodny Komissariat Vnutrennikh Del*, or People's Commissariat of Internal Affairs).

Following a two-year rule, Menzhinsky's fate befell Yagoda. On a trumped-up charge he was accused of treason and after two years in prison with full GPU-NKVD treatment, Yagoda appeared at a show trial, admitting to all kinds of crimes which Party ascribed him. The first edition of Great Soviet Encyclopedia wrote (volume 38, page 82): Vyacheslav Rudolfovich Menzhinsky was *"villainously put to death on the orders of the anti-Soviet right-wing block, by the provocateur and fascist Yagoda aided by fascist doctors unmasked by the Soviet intelligence and convicted by the Soviet Court."*

From 1936 to 1938 the new head was Nikolay Ivanovich Yezhov (1894-1939), who on Stalin's orders unleashed a renewed reign of terror, and who organised the greatest show trials known to the world. For his merits Stalin paid him in kind. He was arrested, tortured and executed as a result of his "confession."

In 1938 a Georgian Lavrenty Pavlovich Beria (1899-1953) was made the new head of NKVD. After Stalin's death he attempted to usurp the power but was checked in time and executed by shooting.

On 13th March 1954 the secret police were renamed yet again, this time they would be called the "KGB."

From 1954 till the coup of 1991 the post of the head of the Committee was occupied by a series of mediocre executioners, like A. Shelepin (1958-61), V. Semichasny (1961-67), Yu. Andropov (1967-82), V. Fedorchuk (May 1982), V. Chebrikov (December 1982), et al.

KGB, no matter what the name, was always a secret organisation, whose secrets were unfathomable by ordinary mortals. We succeeded in obtaining a copy of the KGB Instruction Manual which we are reproducing here in translation. Having got acquainted with it, the public can learn the mentality and understand the activity of KGB which has always been based on the teachings of Lenin and Stalin, according to which any crime can be considered moral and consequently admissible if it is, in their opinion, of use for the working class. One should not forget, however, that as a result of such policy the working class of the richest country in the world after a seventy-some-year experience have hardly anything to eat or anything to put on.

One of the first detachments of the Soviet secret police.

DUTIES OF POLITICAL INVESTIGATORS

This manual contains instructions for rank-and file intelligence agents. Due to the shortage of electronic equipment in Russia, electronic surveillance is practised for important people, big crime and Western tourists and businessmen. It is described in detail in the ***Manual for Electronic Surveillance*** *produced by KGB "for internal use only."*

1. A political investigator ought to be a calm, selfless person devoted to Soviet power. Each case that he begins he should weigh up before starting.

2. He should feel his superiority over the enemy, know the enemy better than he knows himself. This is the guarantee of victory.

A Soviet citizen who does not blindly accept all the KGB and Party political views is considered an enemy. If he does not keep his views to himself, he becomes an enemy of the people. Such individuals are not supposed to be free and usually spend their lives in prisons and hard labour camps. If they become too known before they are discovered as the enemies of the people, they might be lucky to be punished with exile to the West, like Solzhenitsyn, Bukovsky, Zinoviev et al.

3. In his work he should be very secretive, trying to avoid idle conversations and not disclose his affairs before strangers. He should instil this in all working with him. He is to avoid conversations about work in the streets and not even let it appear that they work together.

4. Conversation about service with outsiders is forbidden.

5. On business trips he should conduct himself correctly and modestly, not talk about business but listen and watch what is going on around him.

6. Be careful with servants and couriers. Conduct official conversation with them since the bulk of the information is collected through servants. In a hotel everything should be examined minutely.

> *Officially there are no servants in Russia. The people who do the work of the servants (**prisluga** in Russian) are called **domrabotniki**, i.e. "house workers." All Soviet people earn meagre wages: 200 roubles a month on average. Western tourists get officially 52 roubles for 1 pound. "House workers" are paid less than any other group. So it is not surprising that "house workers" (in reality servants) gladly accept the task of spying on their masters for a few cigarettes or a bottle of beer.*

7. Work notebooks should be kept especially accurately. It is best to keep a record in a cipher of one's own invention. Pages of written information from secret collaborators should be destroyed after their transfer to the registry.

8. One should avoid keeping important documents at home, but if business demands this then they should be kept in a secure place. One should see that not a scrap of paper gets into the wrong place.

For one in charge of political investigation the acquirement of good collaborators is paramount, since the better they are, the better the work. To attract a collaborator it is necessary to come into immediate contact with enemies of the people as often as possible, and while making inquiries to win them to one's side. One should be careful in payment of money so as not to spend government money for a fabrication which the collaborator will gossip about. After making an agreement with a collaborator one should immediately appoint a place to meet and not drag him to the Department so that he would make inquiries or be known.

The title of an "informer" was not very flattering even in Russia. For this reason KGB decided to call their informers "secret collaborators." In a few years this almost neutral label turned into a very shameful, odious and hateful title.

Only the one in charge of investigation should have dealings with a collaborator. Only the Chief of Department, which is dealing with him should know about a collaborator. Business should be conducted so that when liquidation is carried out the collaborator should not be touched. Collaborators should not know each other as this is the beginning of the end.

In the KGB lingo, "liquidation" is a synonym for execution when it refers to people.

One should know how to keep a secret well and not give it out where one should not.

One should warn a collaborator often to be careful and also warn him if he starts to give incorrect information. Collaborators must not have anything on them. If a search is carried out then it is necessary to arrest a large group, say, five of them without consequences including the collaborator, so that he will not be found out. Pass information that is formal for the inquiry and give the informal personally to the one conducting the inquiry.

The collaborators should not visit their neighbours.

Information is checked by cross-questioning or through an intelligence agent. The secret collaborator comes and communicates one thing or another. Then the intelligence agent is sent who establishes everything accurately. Information ought not to go stale but be put into effect as quickly as possible by way of arrests and searches. Information is all written down.

It is good to make one's collaborators write themselves, and then to reprint it in the agency journal in the Department of the corresponding organisation. Payment should be made in such a way that the collaborator is dependent and unable to blackmail. It is essential to take a receipt. Sometimes information received is obtained by way of observing a place, people etc., as when they are speaking about something; this information has to be checked and something done. It is very important to have special agents who could visit where a crowd is forming.

Sometimes information appears through the press and also from official organs. When information is received, one must be calm, investigate and check it. Internal notification is information on activities of one or another anti-Soviet organisation. The collaborator is a person who belongs to the anti-Soviet organisation as a member and gives information to those conducting the investigation.

It sometimes happens that people who are committed to the cause start to give away all the enemies of the people without demanding pay but such cases are rare.

There are two reasons why people can become informers without asking for money: 1) they want to prove their devotion to the party, so that the could advance quicker in their jobs; 2) they want to get the rooms of the people with whom they share a flat or a house. If one tenant goes to prison, the informer-neighbour usually gets a chance to exchange his small room for a larger one of his neighbour's. Due to the unbelievable shortage of housing in Russia, this very successful system of getting greater "living space" or a room with a better view was practiced on a huge scale until a few years ago. Up to 1953 an anonymous letter was sufficient to send an innocent person to prison for life or even to execution.

One should behave circumspectly towards collaborators and not give them a free hand. A collaborator should be put in a definite condition which he is obliged to fulfil; one should know how to put oneself and the collaborator in a definite framework. If you conduct things successfully your work will proceed very quickly. The collaborator is an external figure and revolves in his own milieu; but one should not bypass important information and use it.

Reasons leading to collaboration are as follows:
1) Committed ideological collaboration ranks highest.
2) Personal or family quarrels. A reliable person will do anything.
3) Personal sympathies towards the one in charge of political investigation are especially good if it is a woman concerned, but he should not allow himself to be distracted by excessive sympathy. She can do a lot but one must be extremely careful.
4) Fear of responsibility and punishment.
5) Profit.
6) Revenge.

KGB have always used women in a most amoral way. A British man (Shimansky), working as a Russian translator for the John Brown construction company, had a very nice young niece in Moscow. Knowing that they have ways of convincing a woman to sleep with any man she is told to, KGB gave the poor translator a simple choice: either you give us information during the multi-million pound negotiation with the firm and in exchange we give you your niece as a lover in Moscow, or bear the consequences. Refusing to become a secret collaborator, the translator was unable to obtain an entry visa to the USSR and lost his job in London.

A. Flegon describes in his book on Solzhenitsyn how KGB forced a bride (Larisa) to sleep with an American businessman (Grove International) one week before her wedding so that they could photograph and blackmail the representative of the company active in the military field.

Political investigators can use the method of persuasion for which it is necessary to talk with the prisoner, proposing they confess and indicating the unrealisability of their dream. For such conversations a man should be of all-round development, who would be able to steer the conversation cleverly. One could even pretend to be a conservative in front of the enemies of the people, indicate that the population does not quite correctly understand freedom, but all the same etc. But one must be able to do this skilfully and know how to touch on the secret side of a person. To use this method skill and culture are necessary.

The correctness of an investigation is conditioned by:
1) Knowledge of the psychology and principles of the anti-Soviet-minded.

2) Expedient morally pure investigatory principles.
3) Devotion to the Soviet Regime.

The first is attained by study of the tendencies and teachings of the enemies of the people .

The second is by study of the instructions published by KGB to fight the enemies of the people.

What this means in the KGB lingo and in practice can be seen from the following passage from the world-acclaimed memoirs by Yevgeniya Ginzburg:

"They got at me again. The 'conveyor-belt' system this time. Interrogation without interruption. The interrogators changed but I was there all the time. Seven days without food and sleep. Without even returning to my cell. Well-rested, shaved, they passed before me as in a nightmare. Livanov, Tsarevsky, Krokhichev, Vevers, Elshin and his 'assistant,' Lieutenant Bikchentayev — short, rosy, curly-headed, like a turkey-cock fed on nuts.

The purpose of the 'conveyor-belt' was to undermine the prisoner physically, to exhaust his nervous strength, to break his resistance, to force him to sign what was demanded of him. At first I used to notice the individual differences in the approach of each investigator. Livanov was quiet and collected, as before, and his tone invariably official. He insisted that I should sign the monstrous gibberish in front of me as if it were the most natural, and at the same time insignificant, detail of office routine. Tsarevsky and Vevers always used to shout and threaten. During these performances Vevers would sniff at a white powder — cocaine. Its effect was to make him mock me, as well as threaten.

'Ha-ha-ha! Look what's become of the belle of the

university! Aksyonov [Ginzburg's husband — publishers' note] would not recognise his birdie now! Go on being stubborn a bit longer, and we'll turn you into an old hag. Been in the rubber isolation cell yet? No? Well, that pleasure still awaits you.'

Major Elshin was always imperturbably gallant and 'humaine.' He liked to talk about my children. He had heard that I was a good mother. But it looked as if I had no pity for my children at all. Having inquired why I had become so 'pale,' and hearing that I had been interrogated for four or five days without food or sleep, he was 'astounded.'

'What sense is there in torturing yourself like this, over signing a document? It's a pure formality, all you have to do is sign and then lie down and sleep. Here, on this sofa, if you like. I'll tell them not to disturb you.'

In the 'purely formal documents' it was stated that I had organised a terrorist group in the Tartar Writers Union, and had recruited to my cause a formidable list of Tartar names, beginning with Kari Nadzhimi, then Chairman of the Union.

'So you feel sorry for Nadzhimi? He didn't feel sorry for you, though,' hinted the Major.

'That's for his conscience to decide.'

'What are you, a protestant missionary or something?'

'No. An honest human being.'

Again the Major didn't miss the chance to show his erudition, and gave a little talk on Marxist-Leninist ethics. Honesty is what is useful to the proletariat and the proletarian state.

'It can't be useful for the proletarian state to annihilate its first generation of Soviet Tartar intelligentsia, let alone those who are Party members.'

'We have precise information that these persons

are enemies of the people.'

'Then why do you need evidence from me, in addition to your "precise information"?'

'To help in framing the documents.'

'I can't frame anything I've never heard of.'

'Don't you believe us?'

'How can I believe you when you keep me in prison for no reason without charge, and when you use illegal methods of investigation?'

'What are we doing that's illegal?'

'So as to force me to give false evidence, you haven't let me eat, drink or sleep for days.'

'Go on, eat! They'll bring food right away. Just sign, you're only torturing yourself...'

Lieutenant Bikchentayev always came with the Major now and appeared to be doing his 'practical.' He would stand catching the ends of the Major's sentences and repeating them like a one-year-old starting to talk.

'It's your own fault,' said the Major.

'...fault,' the Lieutenant echoed.

One day, Major Elshin came up with a document about my connection with the Tartar intelligentsia.

'What made a person like you, who knows French and German, start studying Tartar?'

'Because I wanted to do literary work and translating.'

'But it's such a crude language...'

'Is that what you think too, Lieutenant [Bikchentayev is a Tartar surname — publishers' note]?'

The turkey-cock smiled sheepishly and said nothing.

After this prelude, they invited me to sign a document which stated that I had undertaken to arrange 'an unprincipled alliance of the bourgeois nationalistic elements of the Tartar intelligentsia with and on the orders of the Trotskyite central faction.' I ventured:

'Yes, all my life I've dreamt of uniting the Moslem world for the triumph of Islam.'

The Major guffawed, but nonetheless gave me nothing to eat or drink, and did not allow me to sleep.

At that time, I thought my suffering was boundless. But I discovered a few months later that my 'conveyor-belt' interrogation was child's play compared to what they used to do later, from June 1937. They allowed me no food or sleep, but at least I was sitting and not standing up. Sometimes they would give me water out of the interrogator's carafe. They did not use violence. True, Vevers once nearly killed me, but that was under the influence of cocaine, when he was in an abnormal state, and it frightened Vevers himself terribly.

The incident took place probably on the fifth or sixth night of the 'conveyor-belt.' I was already half delirious. They had a habit of seating the prisoner at a distance from the interrogator, in order to exert 'psychological pressure.' Sometimes the distance was the length of the room. This time Vevers put me against the opposite wall and began to bellow his questions right across his large office. He was talking about how long I had known Professor Korbut, who had joined the Trotskyite opposition in 1927.

'I don't remember exactly what year, but I've known him a long time, since before he first voted for the opposition.'

'Wha-a-at!' Vevers, high on cocaine, and inflamed by my persistence, finally went berserk. 'The opposition! You dare to call that gang of murderers and spies an opposition? You bitch!'

The big stone paper-weight from Vevers's desk

hurtled towards me with tremendous force. I only realised what danger I had been in when I saw the gash in the wall an inch from my temple.

Vevers was so frightened that he came across and gave me a glass of water. His hands shook. He and his kind hadn't yet been given permission to kill prisoners under interrogation. He had been carried away a little.

On the seventh day of the 'conveyor-belt' I was taken down one floor to Colonel whose name I can't remember. Here for the first time I was told to stand during interrogation. I kept falling asleep standing up. So they put a guard each side of me, whose job was to continually jolt me awake, repeating 'Wake up!' Suddenly into my consciousness there floated a similar scene from the film 'Palace and Fortress.' This was just how they had interrogated Karakozov [a Russian revolutionary, who on 4th April 1866 unsuccessfully tried to assassinate the Russian tsar Alexander II — publishers' note]: they had forbidden him to sleep too.

Then everything went hazy. Through a thick mist I saw the Colonel's fastidious expression, noticed the revolver lying on his desk, evidently to frighten his prisoners.

I remember that the circles on the wallpaper annoyed me very much. They were the same as in Vevers's office, and danced unendingly before my eyes. I have no recollection of what I replied to that Colonel. I think I mostly stayed silent, repeating from time to time 'I won't sign!' Sometimes he threatened, sometimes he pleaded, promising a meeting with my husband or my children. Then everything started to whirl, and I fell. I was apparently unconscious for so long, that they were obliged to give up their system. I came to on my own bunk. On opening my eyes I saw

Liama's kind face bent over me, wet with tears. Drop by drop she was pouring orange juice into my mouth, which had just been sent in a parcel to Ira.

Soon we heard anxious knockings on the wall. Garei and Abdullin were worried and were asking how I was.

'She's come to. Fine! Give her our love.'

I had time only to think how good people could be, when I was once again called out for interrogation. The conveyor-belt had started up again."

(E. Ginzburg, ***Precipitous Journey****, Flegon Press, London, 1967)*

The most painstaking attention should be given to the correct assimilation of the material by investigators and intelligence agents. The important task of political investigation demands not only knowledge but love for the work. One should present it so that people have available all methods which can bring priceless benefits.

Difference between criminal and political investigation. Criminal investigation is conducted by virtue of crimes committed; it does not anticipate crimes. Political investigation is conducted before the crime is committed and thus has as its aim prevention, to know not only the actual but also the contemplated.

SPECIAL REMARKS ON INSTRUCTION FOR EXTERNAL SURVEILLANCE

Outside surveillance is in itself a responsible and difficult task which an intelligence agent ought to fulfil honestly and conscientiously, not through fear but conscience. He is to accomplish the missions imposed upon him with utter selflessness because he is a servant of the people and fights its enemies.

It is a bad servant who does not carry out the orders of his master. Agents should be devoted to the party and remember one thing at all times: that they are combating their most bitter enemies whom they should not pity.

The work of the intelligence agents often takes place in abnormal conditions. Therefore they should be resilient and strong in spirit, and possess an iron will in order to overcome all the difficulties and privations of their difficult way. An intelligence agent should overcome all the little philistine thoughts that creep into his mind as these act destructively on the mind of someone devoted to the cause.

An agent should be a pure person despite his having to be everywhere where the sores of the present-day society are especially evident, remembering that he serves the great idea of the people.

He should be sparing and economical with money remembering that he ought to watch every kopeck as this is the money of the working people.

In the interests of work it is sometimes necessary to introduce one or another agent into the anti-Soviet organisation. Such intelligence agents should be painstakingly secretive. They should avoid going to arrests and searches, fearing the possibility of their disclosure.

M. V. FRUNZE, Army Commander, inspects the parade in Red Square, Moscow, 7th November 1924. Less than a year later he was forced by KGB to submit to an operation which he did not, nor was supposed to survive.

INSTRUCTION FOR EXTERNAL SURVEILLANCE

EXTERNAL SURVEILLANCE

The objective of external surveillance is to discover involved persons: where they live, what they do, where they go, whom they meet with, what they receive. An intelligence agent should be active, resourceful and modest and always act in a secretive way.

An intelligence agent ought to have helpers among the servants, caretakers, and militia. This makes his work easier.

An intelligence agent should know the town in which he works well. He should be properly literate so that he can make out a good work report. An intelligence agent should in no way reveal his incognito in public. If he does this he ought to be sacked.

§1.

In the aims of discovering persons engaged in anti-Soviet activity and also their flats, houses or visitors having dealings with them and all their connections in general, secret external surveillance is set up called intelligence operations. The intelligence agents carrying out this surveillance are called intelligence agents and the persons they observe are called intelligence objects.

§2.

Through the surveillance of intelligence agents it is possible to discover a whole number of persons that the man under surveillance sees and houses and flats that he visits. A watch can also be set up on such persons and places which in its turn gives still more connections, and thus from one person watched initially a whole network of intelligence surveillance can develop.

§3.

Intelligence agents appointed to one and the same place form a surveillance post. Not less than two intelligence agents are assigned to a surveillance post, one of whom is appointed in charge.

§4.

To reveal by means of external surveillance anti-Soviet criminal activity is a mission of extreme importance demanding from the intelligence agent especial scrupulousness and complete truthfulness in filing his reports and devotion to the Soviet Government. Every inaccuracy in reports leads to a mistaken evaluation of the anti-Soviet activity on the part of the surveillance controller, to measures being taken against this activity which do not correspond to the actual need and thus only aid the success of the anti-Soviet activity.

§5.

Every intelligence agent should remember that his surveillance will only bring benefit when it is carried out secretly and, therefore, he is obliged to conduct himself so as to be unnoticed either by the person under surveillance or by strangers. For safety's sake the intelligence agent should not keep very close to people he is observing, stand for long in one and the same place, stop for long periods in front of shop windows, look around restlessly, peer into the face of the person under surveillance and, in general, not do anything to make the subject pay him attention.

§6.

In the aims of keeping surveillance secret the intelligence agent should dress in accordance with the conditions of his work. In general, he should be dressed so as not to stand out among the public by his costume but to blend in with them. It is quite useful to have at one's disposal several items of headgear in order to disguise oneself somewhat when necessary by changing them.

§7.

Every person who comes under surveillance is given a special name. This name should be short (of one word that should characterise the appearance of the observed or express the impression he creates; and it should enable one to judge whether it relates to male or female). One should not give similar names to several persons under surveillance.

§8.

An intelligence agent appointed to a post should find out accurately the place from which he should pick up the person under surveillance and become familiar beforehand with him by photograph, and also with his habits as, for example, when he normally leaves his house or returns, or how he conducts himself in the street.

The intelligence agent should take up his post well before the person under surveillance goes out. If the time of his exit is unknown it is necessary to be at the post as the general movement on the streets begins.

§9.

The intelligence agent on surveillance should commit to memory well what the person observed does. He should be able to catch peculiarities in his movements quickly, pay attention to how the subject holds his head and arms, how he moves his feet etc., how he behaves on leaving and entering houses (whether he looks back), learn to detect the naturalness and falsities of his manner when meeting with acquaintances (whether he turns aside from them purposely wishing to hide it, whether he gets confused when he meets militia), be able to determine the appropriateness and suitability to the given person of what he wears (whether he is disguised), memorise exactly all the places which he visits.

§10.

The intelligence agent should commit to memory in all detail persons passing through surveillance and know how to describe in detail and exactly each of them (to be able to give a verbal portrait) both as to their personal characteristics (height, hair colour etc.) and in relation to dress.

In memorising the description of personal characteristics one should be guided by the table of characteristics here attached and turn one's attention to those which cannot be changed at will of the observed person, such as height, eyes, nose, limp etc.

On describing uniform one should indicate in detail cloth colour, piping, shoulder straps and button holes.

The knowledge of how to memorize personal objects and describe them exactly comes with experience. To develop this experience one should behave as follows: scrutinising one of the people around, one should stop gazing and make a mental picture, trying to describe in thought the details, and then check by looking at the practice subject.

§11.

To acquaint oneself with the physiognomy of the observed if one has not managed to get acquainted by photographs, one must use bazaars, crossings, public transport etc., as in such places one can peer into the face of the observed unnoticed by the latter. Peering on half-deserted streets should not be done in avoidance of discovery.

§12.

Staying on the spot in expectation of the observed, the intelligence agent should not be conspicuous, and, therefore, one should take advantage of the neighbourhood, using gates, arches, boulevards, squares and front doors for cover or, for continuous surveillance from one and the same place, even inns, teashops, bars and other places of general use from which one may conveniently observe without revealing oneself.

§13.

When the observed person leaves his house, the intelligence agent should be calm and in no way get confused or dart off. If the observed person does not see him, the intelligence agent can calmly continue with surveillance. But if the subject has noticed him it is best for one to remain a little while not changing position and move only when the subject goes on further or turns a corner. When they notice the subject go out and turn in their direction, intelligence agents should quickly figure out how to avoid meeting the observed and do this without fuss and haste, utilising connecting doors, gates, house entrances, shops where they disappear temporarily giving the observed time to pass them and then follow him again. If a meeting is inevitable, the intelligence agent should in no way meet the subject's glance.

§14.

The distance from the intelligence agent to the observed person should be such that the intelligence agent could see everything that the observed is doing, but that the latter could not suspect that he is being watched. If the street is straight, long and deserted the intelligence agent should keep as far away as possible; on busy, lively streets and especially in a crowd they should keep as close as possible. In small, provincial towns where intelligence agents are especially noticeable, the method of parallel surveillance is practised: one of the agents goes down the street parallel to the one the observed is going down at the speed of the observed, while the other agent goes behind the observed but at such a distance from him that he is just visible. The first intelligence agent comes level with the observed in the street crossing where the intelligence agents check the passage of the observed. When observing a very serious subject two agents go down parallel streets: one on the right and the other on the left side of the observed while a third trails him at a considerable distance. When surveillance is carried out in large towns where one cannot stay in one place without attracting the attention of the inhabitants, the observed should be picked up on the move, i.e not from home but on his way from there or on a walk.

§15.

If the observed person has turned the corner it is necessary to increase one's speed to see that the subject does not enter anywhere. On semi-deserted streets this should be done from the opposite side, as on such streets the observed can be seen more conveniently from the opposite side. If the observed turns a corner, to find out the place he has gone to, one of the intelligence agents necessarily ought to find out the nearest connecting courtyards and look whether the subject has passed through them to another street; while another should choose a convenient stopping place from which to observe the houses nearest to the corner behind which the observed person has disappeared.

§16.

If the observed person intends to get on a tram or a bus, one of the intelligence agents should get on with him and the other is recommended to accompany the subject by cab.

If the subject has gone by cab, the intelligence agents should also follow him in a cab. Therefore, the cabbie should only be indicated the direction to go but in no way told to follow the other cab. When one has seen that the observed person has left the cab and entered a house or gone further on foot, one must leave the cab by turning (to escape detection) round the first corner one comes to and continue the surveillance on foot. Sometimes, for example, when there is no corner near, to avoid losing the subject, it is more convenient for one of the intelligence agents to leave the cab on the move and occupy a position and the other to travel further, settle with the cabbie and then return. It is essential to memorise in good time and write down the number of the cab the observed person is using.

§17.

Should the person under surveillance call into any house, the intelligence agent ought to notice the number of the house, the entrances in general, and the entrance in which the subject entered, and investigate its courtyard, i.e. discover all the entrances and whether it is intercommunicating. The agent must know all the through courtways of the town in which he works.

Having carried this out the intelligence agent should write down the numbers of the flats of the entrance into which the observed person has gone.

When observing the house the subject has entered one

must pay attention whether there is a look out near the house watching activities of the militia.

§18.

If the observed person has gone to the theatre, cinema, park or similar place then one of the intelligence agents ought to set out after the observed and the other remain to guard the exit. The agent who has gone in after the subject should notice the cloakroom where the subject has left his coat in order to determine from which exit he will leave. (If the intelligence agent has gone in after the subject he should notice this.)

If the intelligence agent for some reason finds staying in the theatre inconvenient for himself, when he has noted well the characteristics of the person whom the observed person has met, he goes outside and joins his comrade and they await together the exit of the subjects.

If the person observed goes into a cafe or restaurant, the intelligence agent should follow him in as a visitor of that place and take advantage of the buffet to continue surveillance. If as a result of surveillance it is clear that the subject has entered not to meet somebody but simply to eat, drink tea etc., the intelligence agent should go out to join the agent outside. If it is evident that the observed person is waiting for somebody, the intelligence agent should order something for himself to continue surveillance.

§19.

If intelligence agents are conducting surveillance from a cafe, restaurant or similar establishment they should sit so that the observed person is visible when he makes his exit. Money to pay the bill should always be ready. One should avoid conversations with outsiders and not conduct business conversations. On noticing the subject one must calmly finish drinking one's tea, settle up and leave. If the observed person is in a cafe, restaurant etc., it is especially important not to rush off from one's seat after him but to come out a little later, completely calmly and normally.

§20.

If an intelligence agent notices that the observed person is becoming agitated and looks around, he should determine the reason (has he noticed he is being watched or does he want to be noticed as he enters somewhere), and then continue surveillance with especial care and, as the place permits, even going round on foot or in a vehicle.

§21.

If during surveillance a meeting in a flat, park or restaurant is accidentally discovered and the number of such participants is larger than the number of intelligence agents one should immediately contact the Security Bureau to send reinforcements. If the number of observed persons, notwithstanding the reinforcement sent, is still larger than the number of intelligence agents the most serious (very conspirative) persons bearing suspicious packages are taken under surveillance.

Those taken again under surveillance should be accompanied to the place where it would seem from all signs that they live or where they pass the night in order to have the possibility of taking them under surveillance again if it is found necessary. Signs of returning home can be a moderate pace, entering without ringing with one's own key, coming out onto the balcony in casual dress, switching on the lights in the flat, going to buy foodstuffs etc.

"Here I lived till the winter of 1921 at my aunt's house, but in January they again started questioning me what I did in the Novosyolov's band. I was indignant, denied and cursed. They said that I was allegedly seen to take away a horse from a peasant. But mainly it was suspected that I led in tow a band of Whites, who attacked Yaltsevskaya district last night. I was detained; they thought that I directed them. 'The band has already retreated, but we have to send you to the district centre. What they are going to do with you is no concern of ours.' There I was again interrogated. I did not have any papers on me, and so as an obvious spy I was taken to Chesnovskoye village, where the Cheka made away with bandits. They were stuffed in a big ice-hole and drowned, almost without finding out who the person was: for if he found himself in that village it was all clear with him.

They chased me toward that ice-hole. I burst into tears, I got scared. I stood and everything was jumping before my eyes.

There were only two people in front of me, and I started feeling really bad. Well, I thought to myself, by spring I maybe would surface somewhere, not earlier.

Executioner with a verdict on his lap —>

Suddenly I heard them shouting: 'Shabalin, Afanasiy, a heroic partisan, how did you manage to find yourself here?' I looked and saw our former partisans approaching. I rushed toward them and told them everything. They started cursing and took me out of the queue. The partisans confirmed that I was not an enemy and got me released. While they went for the papers, still tied up, I stood by the ice-hole. Now they were drowning three brothers and the father. The first two were drowned quickly, but the third got out, grabbed some fellow and dragged him into the ice-hole with him. That fellow floundered about in water a bit, the comrades saved him, gripped and held him, but could not tear him from the drowning man's hands: he seized hold of the greatcoat so that it was impossible to extricate it. Only when his hands were chopped off, was the soldier released. The father of the drowned brothers first looked at the ice-hole, but then turned away. They pushed him and he went to the bottom without resistance."

A. Shabalin, Twenty Years of My Life, Moscow, Molodaya Gvardiya (Young Guard) State Publishing House, 1931

§22.

If when one person is being observed a meeting is noticed (especially if it bears a clandestine character) between him and other persons, then these latter should be taken under surveillance and accompanied till their dwelling place or where they spend the night is established. Intelligence agents can act as they deem fit as far as elucidation of the subject's identity and exact establishment of their dwelling; in general these elucidations are carried out by someone especially appointed.

§23.

If the intelligence agent cannot leave his post but must report something, e.g. that it is essential to increase manpower etc., he writes a note to the person in charge of surveillance and sends it off by messenger or cabbie, memorising their numbers. The note should be written as prearranged (in such and such a house guests await you, send so many salesmen to such a place, we await you with comrades in such a place, etc.)

§24.

If several persons under surveillance gather in one place and, consequently, crowding of intelligence agents has occurred, the latter should not group but immediately assign roles and leave the necessary number of posts; all the superfluous must go to the nearest covered place (bar, cafe etc.) where to wait for the signal to come out.

§25.

Surveillance of places which are supposed to be sites for arms stores etc., is conducted with extreme care and done from special flats or surrounded by one's own cabbies, traders, messengers etc. to help whom pedestrian intelligence men are assigned. The latter do not stay near the house of the observed person. And blocking the exits of the streets they pick up the observed on the way and watch them with especial care; especially when the subject is returning to his home.

§26.

In places inaccessible for intelligence men on foot and also to observe the most important enemies of the people, surveillance from vehicles is assigned, and carried out by intelligence men disguised as cabbies.

An intelligence man dressed as a cabbie should remember before everything that by appearance he is firstly a cabbie and, therefore, needs the skill to dissemble before the public, militia and other cabbies. He should carry out all demands of the militia without question even though this causes harm to his surveillance. In the last resort the intelligence agent, submitting to the rank of militia, should, unnoticed by other cabbies, speak to the militia asking their cooperation in work interests. He should have recourse to this only in exceptional circumstances.

The agent-cabbie finds it exceptionally difficult not to reveal himself in such cases, when through circumstances of work, he must stop in places where there are no nearby stopping places for other cabs, when in such cases caretakers and watchmen drive away cabbies. Thus he must always have a ready answer to retain his place. What to reply and to whom depends on the resourcefulness of the intelligence agent: to one he can say that he is waiting for one of his clients, to another that he has taken the doctor to a patient, to a third that he has been called and is awaiting a customer, to a fourth he can promise refreshment, etc.

Among other cabbies the agent-cabbie should conduct

himself extremely carefully, converse with them as little as possible and try to behave as if he in no way differs from them. If the observed person tries to hire a cab, the intelligence agent should make excuses not to carry him, stating that he is taken, If it is impossible for him to refuse, he should carry him but necessarily stay on his guard and try to be completely like a cabbie.

§27.

An agent-cabbie normally carries out surveillance using the aid of pedestrian agents. Awaiting the exit of the observed, he usually stands in a place convenient for surveillance, while agents on foot hide in the nearest cover such as a cafe, pub etc. When the observed person makes his exit, the cabbie either moves after him and then takes the pedestrian intelligence agents (if the person under surveillance has gone into a cab) as ordinary clients and follows the subject, or the cabby moves after the observed and the agents on foot follow him. The cabby conveys to the agents awaiting in the cafe or pub that it is necessary to follow the observed person either by a prearranged signal from the street or by the cabbie entering the cafe under some plausible pretext.

§28.

Having lost the observed person, intelligence agents should make every effort to get him again under surveillance; for which they should again begin work from his lodgings or at a place he visits most frequently.

§29.

If the observed person sets off for the station, harbour or airport and there is no instructions as to whether he should be accompanied on his departure, the intelligence agent asks the person in charge of the Intelligence Bureau or, if this is impossible or there is no time, makes the decision by himself. In deciding this question the agent should take into consideration how important the subject is, which is possible to determine through the preceding surveillance: whether the subject has been in the company of important subjects of surveillance, whether he has been visiting flats under intense surveillance, whether he has with him anything that arouses suspicion by weight, size, shape and the way the observed handles it. One should behave in the same way when it is not the observed person who is leaving, but the person whom the observed has gone to escort to station, quay or airport.

If the observed has gone to get a ticket, one should try to stand directly behind him to discover where the ticket to. Failing this, he is to enlist the secret aid of a militia officer or porter.

If he has not been able to discover where the subject has taken the ticket to, the intelligence agent takes a ticket to the first major station and en route finds out where the observed person is going, for which he listens to the conductor or controller who, when examining the ticket, have a habit of speaking aloud the passenger's end station or, in the last resort, gets the information by openly asking.

§30.

Having decided to follow the observed on the railway, the intelligence agent should consider which carriage it is best for him to sit in, which will depend on how calm and wary the subject is. If it is possible he should sit in the same carriage with him occupying some upper berth, but not in the same compartment. On the journey the intelligence agents do not sleep but take turns to observe, especially trying not to miss the preparations of the observed to dismount from the carriage.

§31.

If the observed departs suddenly the intelligence agents should, at the first possibility, telephone the chief of the Intelligence Bureau as to on which train, after whom and where they are travelling, and also indicate a link station where they can be sent a telegram poste restante. If the destination of the subject is known to the intelligence offices they should notify the chief of the Intelligence Bureau by urgent telegram, telex or fax.

§32.

On arrival in a strange town the intelligence agent immediately communicates his address to the chief of the Intelligence Bureau, then reports to the local KGB and acts as they direct.

§33.

The intelligence agent should keep the chief of the Intelligence Bureau informed as often as possible by registered post, telex or fax of the results of the work out of town. Letters are sent in two envelopes sealed with sealing wax, with an incision made in the larger top envelope in the place where the seal is, so that the wax penetrates into the lower envelope and seals it to the one above.

It is recommended to post the letters at large stations. All letters from a single place ought to have the usual serial numbering and indication of when and where they were composed.

§34.

If one is told to arrest the observed person, one must follow him as far as possible away from his flat and arrest him with the aid of the nearest militiamen. During the actual arrest the intelligence agent must be vigilant that the observed has not discarded any objects on the street;

then he arrests him and takes him to the militia station or KGB office.

If he is told to take his prisoner to the militia station, on arrival the agent asks for the prisoner to be searched, and observes that this is carried out as thoroughly as possible, and that the protocol is made exactly indicating everything discovered. Having accompanied the prisoner to the militia, the intelligence officer reports this to the KGB.

§35.

At a set time intelligence agents gather daily to give information about the results of daily surveillance.

At these general meetings intelligence agents exchange details of new persons that entered the sphere of surveillance on the given day and surveillance data in general. And in this way they establish whether a given person has fallen in the sphere of surveillance of another post and assist each other in establishing the places the subject visits.

All that the intelligence agent has noticed in the course of surveillance during the day he is obliged to set out in detail in his notes. Information on every new person that has come under surveillance should begin with a detailed description of his physical traits; then his resident address should be indicated.

In mentioning the places the observed visits, one should indicate exactly beside the street names also the house numbers and the family name of the owner, and likewise where possible the flat, entrance, floor and wing.

If in one location the observed visits two or several places, one should indicate each time where actually they called. In reports one should not indicate "went to see such and such a person" but "visited such and such a house where so and so is resident."

In reports one should stipulate those places which the observed person frequents by necessity (dinner, work, studies, relatives etc.) if already known.

§36.

If intelligence agents meet in the street they should not only not approach each other, but give no sign that they are acquainted. The same should apply to all secret collaborators of the KGB except to office staff. If one wishes to indicate that a conversation is necessary, prearranged signals must be used.

* * *

Nikolay Ivanovich YEZHOV (1894-1939), head of OGPU and NKVD in 1936-38: tête-à-tête with Stalin.

WHAT EVERY OFFICER, INVESTIGATOR AND UNDERCOVER AGENT WORKING FOR INVESTIGATION SHOULD REMEMBER

1. Always be correct, polite, modest and resourceful.

2. Do not shout and be gentle, but know when to show firmness.

Millions of Soviet citizens had an opportunity to get acquainted with the gentleness of KGB investigators. Army general Alexander Gorbatov, an ex-commander of Berlin, met these "gentle" people more than once. In 1964 he published his memoirs in Moscow. At that time KGB was still in power and he tried to describe his experience in a way which would not offend them too much:

"For three days I was not called, but on the evening of the fourth I was taken to the interrogator. He checked my biography and gave me seat, and then handed me paper and pen and proposed that I 'describe my crimes.'

'There is nothing to write about my crimes,' I replied.

'Nothing!' he said. 'They all say that at first, then think things out, remember and write. You have time, there's no hurry. Those who have nothing to write are free, but you shall write.'

He left the room.

The hours passed. Seeing that I had written nothing, the interrogator was surprised.

'What's the matter, don't you understand what is required of you? Bear in mind that we don't like jokes, get on with it! It is not to your advantage to spoil

Genrikh YAGODA (1891-1938),
head of NKVD in 1936-38.

relations with me. I have never had a case when someone has not written. Understand?'

He again left the room.

About an hour later, on seeing that I was still not writing, the interrogator said:

'You have behaved badly from the very beginning. A pity! Well then, think it out in your cell.'

Two stalwart jailers locked me up in the cell. As soon as the door had slammed behind me, I was inundated with questions: 'What did they ask? What did you say? What did you testify?'

Having heard me out, they concluded that the method of interrogation had not changed. I would have to wait for later calls, when I would begin writing or they would take me to Lefortovo.

This forecast was confirmed. A day later, when the same thing occurred as at the first interrogation, the interrogator behaved extremely crudely, swore and threatened to send me to Lefortovo. The same day I was called again for a short period. This time a person of higher rank spoke to me. He proposed that I should testify, and on hearing my firm refusal also began to swear and concluded with the threat, 'You'll be sorry!'

The next day the cell door opened and a man entered and asked:

'Anyone here with surname beginning with G!'

I gave my name. It was clear to all that I was going to be taken to the prison at Lefortovo. They commiserated with me, gave me advice and wished me all the best.

I sat in a black and impersonal vehicle, heard the engine start up and the gates clang shut. Now and again speech and laughter in the streets reached my ears. Then I heard the gates of the Lefortovo prison open and shut. I finished up in a small cell once for solitary prisoners. There were already two occupants. Three beds stood against three of the walls.

My neighbours were brigade commander B., and K., head of a Chief Committee of the People's Trade Commissariat [Ministry of Commerce — publishers' note]. Both had already written nonsense about themselves and others in the belief that they had no other alternative. Their accounts sent shivers down my spine. I could not believe that such things could happen here. It was the opinion of my new colleagues that it was better to write straight away, since if you did not sign today, you would still sign in a week's time or in six months.

'I would rather die,' I said, 'than slander myself and, all the more so, others.'

'We felt the same way when we landed up here,' they answered.

Three days passed. The interrogator began calling me. At first the interrogations differed little from those in the Lubyanka. Growing certain that I would not write, the interrogator hissed, 'You'll write. We have never had, and never shall have, anybody who did not!'

On the fourth occasion I was called by one of the chiefs. First he asked me calmly whether I understood what I was letting myself in for, whether I had thought things out well and weighed things up. Then this chief told the interrogator, 'Yes, I agree with you!' and left the room.

On that occasion a long time passed before my return from interrogation.

When with difficulty I reached my cell, my comrades said in one voice:

'There! and that's only the beginning.'

Comrade B., shaking his head, asked me quietly, 'Is all that necessary?'

Alexander GORBATOV,
Army General, ex-commander of Berlin,
Hero of the Soviet Union.

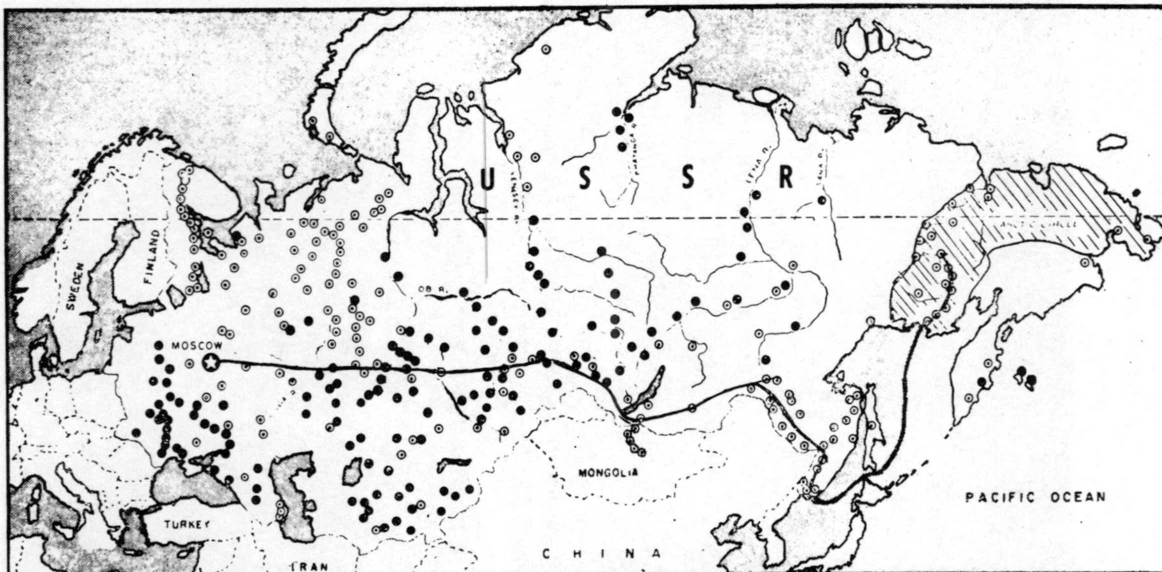

Gorbatov's route to slave labour in Kolyma gold mines. Each dot on map stands for a forced-labour camp.

There were five trials by ordeal at two or three day intervals; there were occasions when I had to be helped back to the cell. Then they gave me about twenty days to recover. I was most concerned about my wife. Then suddenly I received 50 roubles, and this gave me cause to believe that she was free. My cell mates thought that the respite in the interrogations was a good omen for me.

However, they soon began calling me to interrogation again, and there were again five periods. During one of them I learnt by chance that the name of my monster of an interrogator was Stolbunsky. I do not know where he is now. If he is alive, I would like him to read these lines and to feel my loathing for him, not only now, but when I was in his hands... I think in any case that he knew it full well. Besides the interrogator, two toughs were present during interrogation. I can still hear Stolbunsky's sinister hissing voice, 'You'll sign, you'll sign' as they carried me out, broken down and bloody. I withstood this torture through the second series of interrogations, but when the third series began, how I wished I were dead!

Once Comrade B. asked me: 'Doesn't this convince you that your position is hopeless?'

'No, it does not,' I replied. 'I shall die, but I shall still say no and no again!'

(A. Gorbatov, ***Black Year****, Moscow and London)*

3. Think before you speak.

4. Be prudent during searches, do not court disaster, be polite, exact and punctual.

5. Always be polite with the public but firm where needed.

6. Be tidy and clean so that your appearance disposes people towards you and gives you the chance to find out something from them.

7. Each agent should remember that he is called upon to protect Soviet State and not to allow transgression against it. If he himself does not behave accordingly, he is an unworthy person and should be removed from the ranks of the Committee of State Security.

8. One should always remember the characteristics of the Jesuits, who did not proclaim their work from the housetops, nor exhibited it for everyone to see. Rather they were strange people who knew about everything and knew how to act.

The critics of Marxism often compare the status of Marxism in communist states to that of religion, much to the displeasure of the Marxists in those states. Here we have the communist watch dogs make the same allusion.

9. Be pure and incorruptible because a mercenary bent is betrayal of the Workers' and Peasants' State and of the people in general.

10. Be consistent and steadfast, know how to get your bearings quickly, adopt wise measures so that enemies cannot laugh, mocking your ideological poverty. There should be no place for wilfulness in this service.

11. If you discover negligence and abuses somewhere, do not make a big commotion as this will injure the cause; but it will be laudable if you catch them red-handed and then lead them to a pillory.

12. Guard the orders given you like the apple of your eye.

INSTRUCTION
FOR FIGHTING PROFITEERING

One of the most necessary measures to restore the domestic economic life of the country which has been shattered by relaxation of laws, is fighting rampant profiteering both in foodstuffs and objects of first necessity due to which, no matter how high the earnings may be, life for poor people becomes progressively more difficult. Any method of fighting, no matter how indecent it might seem to us, the socialists, can be applied to profiteers and the enemies of the people. One can say from the experience that the only principle in the war with profiteers and enemies of the people is that the end justifies the means.

One must confess that the capitalists have an excellent apparatus for tracking down and catching persons damaging to their interests. The necessity of such admission, in our view, obliges us, in the name of the further achievements of the October Revolution, to create a much better apparatus of fighting which would in the interests of the people engage in the neutralisation and persecution of those criminal elements which undermine at the root the whole economic life of the country. Of course, talking about the organisation of such an apparatus of fighting, one should in no way suppose that it is necessary to employ the same elements as in the capitalist model. No, on the contrary, while their capitalist counterparts do the dirty work for money, those employed in our apparatus do it because they are vitally interested in the destruction of all that hinders their free life the development of the first workers' and peasants' state. From the teachings of Marx, Engels and Lenin we know that our cause is just and the hostile forces will not succeed. For this purpose the KGB Department for Fighting Profiteering was formed and recently expanded as profiteering, or "racketeering" as it is called now, had soared to unacceptable levels due to "perestroika."

The Department is divided into two sections:
1. Intelligence
2. Technical

The intelligence section is engaged in the discovery of existing profiteer organisations or rackets, exposure of their criminal activities, investigation of goods hidden in warehouses, railway depots and flats, surveillance of all places where profiteers gather, etc. For this aim the intelligence section will be granted the widest powers in tracking down, catching and arrest of persons they deem necessary. It is necessary to keep the population and our social organisations informed of the existence of this type of intelligence so that their help and co-operation is secured in fulfilment of our obligations.

For the successful work of the intelligence section a method is necessary which we can only regard with repugnance. Speaking openly this method is fighting by means of fiction, or more simply fighting by provocation.

People intended for this aim should be obligatorily and absolutely of impeccable honesty, devoted to struggle for the people's interest, fully prepared to be investigators, properly literate and with knowledge of the commercial world and all the dealings of the world of profiteering.

Each of these employees should be considered secret so that he does not give himself away immediately and, therefore, his collaboration in the department should be secret even for the members and other employees of the department. Nor is it permissible for him to figure in legal procedures.

The work of the secret employees ought to be divided into several sections, for fighting will go on far more effectively if each of the employees has before him a definite goal of fighting one section of trade. This also gives the possibility for employees to specialise and make a good study of the market. Besides which it would be very desirable if it were possible to recruit employees from those establishments and enterprises where profiteering takes place as e.g. railworkers, employees of food establishments, collective and state farms etc. There is also a necessity to have secret employees on the telegraph, telex, fax and telephone stations as these serve as a good means of intercepting and also to discovering lines leading to dens of profiteers. A certain sum of money should be assigned to secret employees for them to conclude fictitious deals or create joint ventures with western firms, and also a certain quantity of western clothing as appropriate to a given deal and required for our new conditions.

Each of the secret employees ought to be issued also several fictitious documents so that he could do deals as director of a co-operative or free enterprise, representative or a buyer of a firm, etc.

One person who would be in charge of this secret intelligence should keep all the above listed.

The person in charge of secret intelligence, who does not carry out any operations himself, should be conversant with the work of secret employees. Moreover he should be given the right to sanction his veto on one or the other work or project undertaken by employees: he should also have monitoring functions. The widest powers in the control of secret employees' activity are necessary, including the arrest of employees if there is sufficient basis for it. The head is given an assistant with the same powers to help him.

Secret Intelligence should have its own secretary who also knows everything going on but does not have those rights which the head and his assistant possess. Here are three persons of Secret Intelligence whose responsibility is to carry on all investigation in the field of profiteering.

* * *

Soviet marshals (left to right): Tukhachevsky (murdered), Budyonny (survived by murdering his colleagues), Voroshilov (survived by murdering his colleagues), Bluecher (murdered) and Yegorov (murdered).

RIGHTS AND DUTIES OF INTELLIGENCE SECTION

The head of the agency and also all agents should keep informed about measures carried out by the central government and large municipal centres in the field of prices, stocktaking, rationing of goods and products, as well as about market prices for all that is on sale both by profiteers and at regulated prices. Participation of the head of intelligence is also necessary with the right of a deciding or consultative voice as far as possible at all meetings in exchange departments and other food and economic organisations where measures of exchange and provision are discussed. These same demands, although in different degree, are required of the assistant head and agents.

Persons of both sexes are accepted as agents, being of no less than 25 years of age, experienced in investigation, energetic, possessing normal sight and hearing, attentiveness, visual memory, quick-witted,able to weigh circumstances, well-developed, properly literate, not of too conspicuous exterior, having pledged to submit to all the rules of the agency, who have successfully passed the training school for agents, had practical investigatory experience and taken the corresponding examination.

Agents must know the layout of streets in the town where they work, be good at map reading, constantly have at their disposal maps, a watch and a guide of all establishments and persons able to afford them help.

Names of persons working in the agency should in the interests of the work remain secret as far as possible, i.e. not leak into the press, not figure as witnesses in legal cases unless under special necessity and, in general, remain known only to the Economic Committee of the KGB.

All agents should be Komsomol or Party members and their personal interests be devoted to the work, and they should always be ready to carry out these or other tasks laid on them by the Soviet authority.

Agents not adequate to their job are dismissed from service without right of appeal.

All agents should know each other by sight and offer each other help without delay.

A constant close link between the head of Agency and agents is necessary (at any time of day and night).

Agents' circle of activity is limited to the fight against profiteering and only in exceptional cases can they deviate from this.

In respect of profiteers agents are given power to arrest and conduct searches and seizures as far as possibility allows, immediately informing the head of the Agency. Searches and arrests must be conducted with utmost caution and used, for the time being, in extreme circumstances.

Agents immediately communicate about all their activities and measures in the form of a report on their daily work to the head of the Agency.

The day's agenda and rota of agents are assigned at the discretion of the head of the Agency.

Agents should submit their addresses and a photograph to the head of the Agency and his assistant (controller) whom they should not know by sight.

For service reasons agents have the right to receive a pocket firearm and have unrestricted free passage on all types of transport without having to wait in a queue.

For active operations, e.g. raids on shops, warehouses, restaurants, and similar places, the necessary number of Committee men is called working under the instruction of agents.

In respect of persons belonging to the Agency, if they are detected in service-related crimes, the most severe measures should apply as to crimes most serious.

The reward of agents is received in three forms: salary, "separate" pay and commission (percentage pay); percentage and piece reward are determined dependent on the complexity and effectiveness of the work by the presidium of the Agency together with the head of the Agency.

All salaries to be considered but provisional in view of the high cost of living in Moscow.

Besides salary, expenses incurred in the fulfilment of service obligations are paid separately, on presentation of bills where possible. This may be, in case of necessity, travel in pursuit of a departing profiteer in the town, rail and air travel, expenses in visits to restaurants and hotels with the aim of getting acquainted with profiteers, per diem expenses for assignments beyond the limits of the town.

The Department ensures that agents receive clothes, cloth etc. for disguise necessary to the successful outcome of investigation.

* * *

General ROKOSSOVSKY, Hero of the Soviet Union, who like millions of innocent victims was tortured by Soviet police.

TECHNICAL SECTION

The head of the Agency stands also at the head of the Technical Section.

1. On receiving information from an agent on the necessity of an arrest, search, revision or seizure, the head of the Agency writes the corresponding request empowering the agent to carry out the said operation.

2. In the request it should be specified by whom the intelligence was supplied on the grounds of which the said operations are being carried out, who is responsible for its correct fulfilment, and exactly where it is to be conducted.

3. On presentation to the general secretariat of the Committee of the request signed by the head of the Agency and his secretary, the agent who received the assignment to fulfil the given operation, receives a corresponding warrant authorising him to carry it out.

4. To ensure the operation's greater success, it is highly desirable that the agent who supplied the information on the basis of which the given operation is being conducted, controlled it.

5. It would also be desirable that the investigator who is to be in charge of the case in connection with the operation, was present while it was being conducted. Also the presence of an expert or simply a leading figure of the branch to which the given operation appertains, would be no less expedient.

6. On receiving the warrant, the officer in charge brings with him a sufficient quantity of armed force from the

detachment attached to the Committee; while he beforehand sets a strict order of the conduct of the operation.

7. With each warrant received one must obligatorily go to the corresponding district militia department, so that they could send a representative to be present during the search and give all possible assistance.On arrival to the militia department, the holder of the warrant should not say in what house and what flat number the search will be carried out, but mention only the street and request a person from the militia to accompany the KGB agent to conduct the search. If the operation cannot be delayed, one can communicate with the militia by telephone in the following manner: "In your district a search will now be carried out on such and such a street" and that is all.

8. During the conduct of the operation representatives both of the house administration and of the district militia should be obligatorily present.

9. While the search, revision or seizure is carried out the KGB officer assigns all the people at his disposal to a particular task according to especially worked out instructions for each operation.

10. During the search attention should be paid to all details, and all trivia. Moreover, it should be pointed out to those carrying out the search that everything present in the area being searched can have its own essential importance. At the same time it should be pointed out that places where the significant for the inquiry evidence may be concealed are extremely varied.

11. While the search is carried out, it is undoubtedly necessary to pay the most serious attention to the correspondence discovered. It may also be useful to

examine or remove photographs. In general, during a search, each trifle, each at first glance insignificant item has its value and significance; and only by unbending following of a strictly defined system, a strictly established method, can one come to the conclusion that everything possible has been done for the proper search for evidence against the criminal.

12. Examining thoroughly all material evidence, what is needed is taken for attachment to the investigation file.

13. Large sums of money should also be removed, gold in ingots and in coins, silver in ingots and coins, foreign currency personal documents (in case of an arrest), extracts from ledgers, cheques, promissory notes and other material of value to the investigation.

14. Under no circumstances should articles of domestic use, small sums of money, foodstuffs in small quantity in accordance with special instructions and other things and objects of no value to the investigation be removed.

15. During the conduct of the search all present in the given dwelling are subjected to a personal search and no one is allowed out of the dwelling. All those who arrive at the given dwelling are allowed in. During the search conversation on the telephone or conversations in an unknown language are also not permitted.

16. When a search is being carried out on a foreign national the corresponding embassy must be informed through the Ministry of Foreign Affairs.

17. On completion of a search all the details are entered in a protocol, in which it must be necessarily specified how the search was conducted, what has been removed, what has been sealed, who has been arrested etc.

18. The resident of the flat and also those present should sign the protocol and in the case of anybody refusing, the officer in charge should enter the fact in the protocol and arrest him.

19. The resident of the flat and also those present have the right to make notes on the protocol of all irregularities committed during the search if the officer in charge agrees with them.

20. During the search all personnel should behave as befits good party members.

21. Everything removed by the officer in charge (goods, valuables and money) should be conveyed to the Depository, and material evidence and confiscated materials to the duty officer of the department in exchange for the corresponding receipt.

22. Arrested persons after preliminary questioning are handed to the prison governor.

* * *

Honorary Certificate of the meritorious NKVD officer Ivan Grigoryevich Zaytsev together with the badge given over to the English publishers. Under the photograph and signature of the owner, the certificate reads:
"The Chekist must be: selflessly devoted to the Party of Lenin-Stalin, watchful and merciless in the struggle with the enemies of the Soviet state."
In addition to their true and sinister purpose, presently such certificates are used in the Soviet Union to intimidate sales and service personnel into service and to obtain various small advantages, such as getting some place without standing in a queue. --->

м. п.

Подпись владельца И. Зайцев

ЧЕКИСТ ДОЛЖЕН БЫТЬ:
БЕЗЗАВЕТНО ПРЕДАННЫМ
ПАРТИИ ЛЕНИНА—СТАЛИНА,
БДИТЕЛЬНЫМ
И БЕСПОЩАДНЫМ В БОРЬБЕ
С ВРАГАМИ СОВЕТСКОГО
ГОСУДАРСТВА

НКВД СССР

ГРАМОТА

Товарищ Зайцев
Иван Григорьевич
приказом
НКВД СССР № 468
от 7 июля 1943 г.
награжден нагрудным знаком
Заслуженного работника НКВД
№ 2599 за успешную
работу по выполнению
заданий

Народный комиссар
внутренних дел Союза ССР Л. Берия
(Л. Берия)

„30" августа 1944 г.

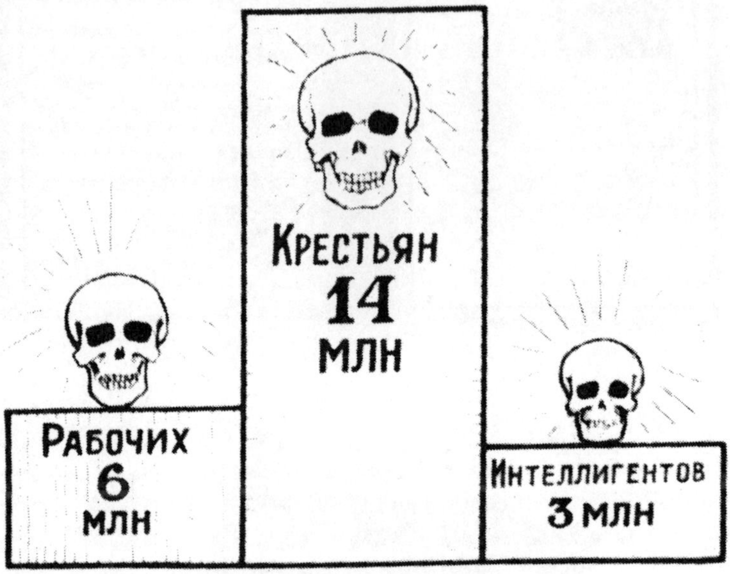

In the years of Stalin's collectivisation and repressions of 1929-1940 6 million workers, 14 million peasants and 3 million intelligentsia perished in camps, died from starvation or were executed by shooting. This equals the total population at that time of such countries as Belgium, Denmark, Hungary and Norway put together, that is 23,000,000 people in all.

Classified

INSTRUCTION ON CLOSURE, SEALING AND REVISION OF STORES AND WAREHOUSES

1. On arrival to the site, some of the agents or inspectors visit the office of the store, some go to the workers of the enterprise.

2. Agents visiting the office, dependent on the volume of paperwork there, should seal everything or remove for proof of criminal activity books, documents, correspondence and papers.

3. Agents visiting the workers of the enterprise, should remove from them vouchers of receipt and issue, orders about issue and receipt of goods, and also invoice books.

4. The inspector who has a warrant must immediately interrogate both the chief of the store and the enterprise workers.

5. The following questions should lie at the basis of the interrogation:

1) Are all goods entered?
2) Have they all being passed through the books?
3) From where did they come?
4) Where were they being sent to?
5) Were they entered at stock taking?

6. Dependent on the interrogation detain one or several persons.

7. After this it is, in general, necessary to determine with the help of a party-devoted worker what brands are in the store and in what quantity. Write all this in the protocol.

8. After this examine the ledger and compare whether it contains the brands entered in the protocol. If not, then mark these brands in the protocol and approximately determine their quantity.

9. After this the stores and gates are sealed, a signed statement is taken from the enterprise workers that they will not permit anything to be removed without the permission from KGB. When for some reason or other it is inconvenient to seal the store to prevent disruption of the apparatus of exchange, the inspector takes from the manager of an enterprise or the person in charge of the store a signed statement that such and such goods can be sold, but that they undertake obligation not to sell the goods entered in the protocol until the case is investigated by KGB.

10. The inspector going to make a revision of the store must know the whole truth of the matter.

11. He must check according to the list drawn up whether the stock book is correct, how much stock is in it. Attention must be paid to stock not mentioned in the stock book.

12. After which starting from approximately six months back, he takes remnants of stock according to the stock book and begins to check, according to vouchers of receipt and issue, how many goods have been sent out and received. Moreover, absolutely all vouchers must be entered in the stock book.

13. The examination is as set out in paragraphs 3 and 4. Having copied out all the differences, the inspector should note from the vouchers from where goods have come and where they have been sent. After which he goes to the Board or Main Ledger.

14. In the main office the inspector demands documents. He must pay attention to whether the goods were present at stocktaking and when the goods were put for stocktaking. He must also demand documentary proof whether goods were bought or sold on an illegal basis. If the inspector has found that there are goods in the store which are not mentioned in the stockbook, he must ask why and also demand documentary proof.

15. According to the inspector's list of where goods from the store were sent and where released, he checks by documents in the main office whether they have actually been sent, on a legal basis or not, etc.

16. Having collected all the data of his revision, he composes on this basis a report.

LAVRENTY PAVLOVICH BERIA (1899-1953), head of NKVD. His life was dedicated to torture, executions and sex with children and virgins. He chose the victims himself from the streets of Moscow or any other town where he happened to be.

"I saw a predatory hawk-like face of Beria muffled in a scarf, when he pressed himself against the window of the car creeping along the pavement in search of a next female. After this the same man addressed the people speaking with pathos about communism."
(YEVGENY YEVTUSHENKO, Autobiography,
Flegon Press, London, 1966)

In memoirs of women who had dealings with KGB in the post-war years, a dwarf investigator is mentioned more than once working in one of Moscow offices. When beautiful women came to see him, especially from educated and well-to-do circles, to petition him on behalf of an arrested brother, sister, husband or son, he always behaved in much the same way. He made them lick his boots and then perform oral sex on him. After satisfying his ego and his body, he let these women send the imprisoned relative a parcel or to receive a letter from their loved one.

DRAWING AND TEXT BY A SOVIET HARD-LABOUR CAMP INMATE

ATTENTION, CULT!!! In 1938-39 the NKVD Minister L. P. Beria gave orders to reduce the number of inmates not by letting the innocent go free, but by means of destruction of those whom the medical examination showed to be sick with dysentery from the hard labour and undernourishment...

In Kolyma camps of "Dalstroy" (Far East Building Enterprise) the sick and the weak were washed in the bath house and then, under the pretext of being handed out clothing, naked and sweating from the steam, they were driven out in the minus 50 degree Centigrade frost through a second exit into a cage fixed on tractor sledges, carried to the marshes, where the corpses were unloaded with steel hooks. In this way hundreds of thousands of inmates were "reduced."

DEPARTMENT
FOR FIGHTING PROFITEERING

INSTRUCTION

OBLIGATORY RESOLUTION

1. On arrival, the place, be it a flat, store etc., is occupied by an armed detachment.

2. On occupation of the dwelling, a member of the House Committee and the senior caretaker are called to be present during the search.

3. The search and seizure is carried out by the person who presents the warrant or on his orders by someone from the detachment.

4. During the search all documents, books and correspondence relating to profiteering deals, addresses of other persons, visiting cards etc. are removed at discretion.

5. Both firearms and steel arms should be unconditionally removed; likewise cartridges.

6. Money should be removed during the search.

7. Any quantity of foreign currency is to be removed.

8. Food products are removed according to the instruction of the Council of Ministers.

9. All gold should be removed: in coins, in articles and ingots.

10. Silver in ingots and coins should be removed.

11. All goods hidden for reasons of profiteering should be removed and if they are in large quantity, they should be sealed with the wax seal of the Department.

12. Separate articles of an inexpensive or domestic character should not be removed during a search, as also small quantities of foodstuffs.

13. Samples should be removed during a search as material evidence.

14. After a search a protocol is drawn up which is signed by the holder of the warrant, a member of the House Committee or the caretaker and the resident of the dwelling.

15. On arrival in the department, money and gold and silver in ingots are handed to the head of the storeroom who signs for them in the protocol, and at night, to the duty officer.

16. Documents, samples and protocol are handed in the investigatory collegium of the department to the head of the department; in the evening a copy of the search protocol is presented.

17. Everything removed during the search is accurately given to the head of the storeroom and appropriation of any of it is forbidden.

18. The given instruction is absolutely binding for all.

19. Persons who violate this instruction for the first time are handed over to the tribunal of the fellow workers; the

second time after a warning they are dismissed and handed to a military tribunal.

20. Everybody should have a copy of this resolution.

21. Each detained person is subject to a thorough search.

Unanimously accepted by the General Meeting.

* * *

TATTOO OF A SOVIET PRISONER

Cannibal of the 20th century. Death to any opposition!

National-Socialist — Nazi
HITLER
SUPERPATRIOT

Khmer Rouge of POL-POT

STALIN — a member of RSDRP-VKP(b)
(Russian Socialist-Democratic Workers' Party —
All-Union Communist Party of Bolsheviks)

CHAMPION MURDERER RIBBONS: HITLER -- 9 mln, STALIN -- 23 mln, and POL-POT -- 3.5 mln people.

INSTRUCTION OF THE COUNCIL OF FIVE

The following should be requisitioned from private persons and shops if above the established quota: meat, meat conserves, ham, veal, mutton, corned beef, lard, dairy and drawn butter, cotton, linseed, sunflower and mustard oil, eggs, Dutch cheese, onions, dried vegetables, potatoes , cabbage soup and borshcht, potato wheat and rye flour, semolina, buckwheat, pearl-barley, peas, lentils, vermicelli, sugar, tea, honey, treacle, raisins, chocolate, candy, jam, mushrooms, tobacco, large consignments of matches, candles, soap, bran, oats, barley, wheat, oil cakes, shoes, leather, kerosine, fuel oil, petrol, coal.

For food establishments, restaurants and cooperatives a weekly norm is issued. The remaining quantity goes to the regional inventory. Dutch cheese, curd, soured cream, poultry, wildfowl, salmon caviar, potatoes and vegetables are exempted.

Tax on the above-mentioned products will be published by the corresponding authority.

On establishment of profiteering, goods are confiscated and the owner of the goods is handed to the court.

For registry of perishable and other products, we request managers of sealed premises visit the Committee at 2, Dzerzhinsky St., from 10 to 5 p.m. daily.

Copy.
Top Secret.

BRIEF INSTRUCTIONS ON INTELLIGENCE

Section I
GENERAL INSTRUCTIONS

Top secret intelligence received from an environment under investigation is called secret intelligence. A person living in the said enviroment or closely associated with it, and passing secret information is called a secret collaborator. This person remains a secret collaborator as long as his investigatory work is completely unknown to the investigated circles.

If a person gives secret information openly when questioned he will not be a secret collaborator but just an open declarant.

Note. Undercover agents ought not to be confused with secret collaborators, as undercover agents establish connections in the street and, generally, outside the inner life of an anti-Soviet organization under investigation; while the secret collaborator investigates exclusively the inner life of the organisation.

Inner top secret and constant intelligence forms the main and single basis of the investigation of anti-Soviet organisations; and its task is the investigation of criminal anti-Soviet organisations and gathering of incriminating evidence in order to bring them before the court or tribunal in times of Martial Law.

All remaining means and powers of the investigatory organ are just auxiliary. These include:

1) Undercover agents and in the regional and district investigatory agents who, as official figures, conduct elucidation and questioning but secretly "under a plausible excuse."
2) Undercover agents of external surveillance who, by conducting external surveillance develop and check the information of internal intelligence.
3) Chance declarants and members and employees of different government establishments.
4) Anonymous denunciations and popular rumour.
5) Material obtained during searches, distributed appeals, the anti-Soviet press, etc.

One should always bear in mind that a single, even weak, secret collaborator present in the enviroment investigated will give incomparably more surveillance material for discovering anti-Soviet crime than the society in which heads of investigation can circulate.

What society gives will always become the property of the investigatory organ through the official figures with whom heads of investigation constantly come into contact, but internal intelligence on anti-Soviet groups has great significance.

Section II
ACQUISITION OF INTERNAL INTELLIGENCE

The acquisition of secret intelligence is the main concern not only of the one in charge of the investigation, but of all his helpers and collaborators. To acquire secret collaborators, constant and prolonged conversation with the arrested and also their relatives and acquaintances coming to the committee for various reasons, is required.

For this same aim on frontier posts the Committee one must speak personally with all suspicious passengers detained on the frontier if a convenient chance arises.

On the railways and in the airports, transport officers must personally conduct inquiries with railway and airport agents from whom it is necessary to acquire collaborators.

Amongst arrested persons one can acquire collaborators by planting one's own suitable man. Entering into their confidence, he can consequently get his cell mate to be frank. This method has given important results when one's own men have been planted amongst serious criminals.

Conversation should be conducted as a serious discussion, without jokes and familiarities, and always tête-à-tête. Practice had shown that a person may be disposed to work as a secret collaborator on the following basis:

1) Interest one with full rehabilitation if compromising material found in searches or from agency intelligence is present.
2) Influence by persuasion.
3) Make use of disagreements in the group and quarrels

between individual important figures.

4) Interest materially; but inclining to collaboration, one should not promise more than can be given.

One should gain full confidence from the very beginning as this is a considerable token of successful work. Those who can be used best: those being or about to be tried for anti-Soviet activity, single people in difficult material circumstances, those arrested for crossing the frontier in the dark, those arrested with evidence, those subject to exile or deprivation of residence rights, etc.

If a collaborator is acquired from among those arrested, he must have his release arranged so as not to incur suspicion in the anti-Soviet groups; an escape can be simulated.

It is recommended that the person intended should be secretly detained in the street and taken immediately for discussion with the person in charge of the investigation. One should resort to this method if there is sufficient evidence to detain the above-mentioned person fully if results are negative. Such a person can be freed if he will give immediate information establishing the guilt of others. He cannot be freed on a promise that information will be given subsequently.

If agreement is reached with an arrested person, the whole group of people with whom he is, should be arrested as otherwise the group will escape from surveillance.

Inclining a collaborator to work, it should be explained to him convincingly that there will be constant work for him and the advantages which can be derived from investigatory work should be pointed out.

Until a person is fully inclined to work, he should not in any case be acquainted with the methods at the disposal of the intelligence.

There should be no mention made of secret addresses which are given only later when one has full confidence in the collaborator.

It is quite useful to interest prison governors in the acquisition of internal agents, as their work puts them in contact with an element of interest for criminal investigation. In the matter of investigation and acquisition of internal intelligence only a method of incentive will give the best results.

> *From a letter of B. Dyakov to the Minister of State Security of the USSR.*
>
> *"I am now imprisoned for two years, not having committed any crime against the Party or the Soviet state either by word, deed or thought. I am among my enemies in the alien and oppressive atmosphere. Sometimes it seems that all of this is happening in some terrible delirium... In 1937 together with G. N. Melnikov and F. I. Terentyev, the false witness for my case, six other staff members of the "Stalingrad Pravda" were arrested. Then the same accusation was brought against them as against me 12 years later. Then, as with me, Melnikov and Terentyev were accusing them of belonging to an editorial Trotskyist group. These six people were investigated for two years, and in 1940 they were released and rehabilitated in their jobs and in the party. The enemy's slander was exposed. They are completely informed of how the materials on the basis of which I am sentenced appeared in 1937...*
>
> *You know that the enemies of the people presiding*

in 1937 in the top organisations of Voronezh and Stalingrad regions widely advertised themselves as faultless bolsheviks. I was not alone to believe in their devotion to the Party; I was not the only one not to recognise in them two-faced Januses. You also know that at times they demonstratively and hypocritically showed themselves to be leaders of initiative. But that was a screen behind which it was easier to hide their enemies' faces... I must say that fortunately I never fawned on those in charge of the region. I did not write one sycophantic article in the newspapers, although Vareykis and Shver and those with them as best they could inflated their authority, planting the cult of their own worship. But to these ends they did not resort to the help of the local journalists, but used known Moscow writers, even now enjoying prominent positions in the Writers' Union. If necessary I can offer more detailed testimony. But whether these writers had or not criminal relations with Vareykis or Shver, such information I could not have had nor have.

I will not hide that I also was deceived by all this noisy broadcasting about Vareykis as allegedly big party boss. But still I repeat that in spite of all of that, I never sang praises to him. On the contrary, the circumstances had it that, without suspecting it, I often administered him a bitter pill and once I almost paid with my life for this.

Undoubtedly many residents of Voronezh and Stalingrad still remember this. Here are the facts:

1) In 1934 I selected for publishing some materials which harshly criticised the situation of the livestock breeding in the region. In particular they unmasked the saboteur activities of a number of veterinary personnel guilty of excessively high cases of cattle and pig plague. The director of the editorial office G. N. Melnikov shelved the materials. On these grounds we quarrelled and I filed an application with the editor-in-chief demanding to release me of my duties on the editorial staff. Shver suggested a compromise: to forward the materials for evaluation to the director of the veterinary department Viktorov (who, as was known in the editorial office, enjoyed authority with Vareykis). I declared that in that case I would pass the materials on to "Pravda." Then Shver ordered them to be printed. Soon after Viktorov was arrested and sentenced to the highest degree. As was learnt out later, these materials were used as evidence against him.

2) On 11th January 1936 "Stalingrad Pravda" printed my satirical article, levelling a blow against Vareykis's henchman Trotskyist Budnyak, director of the "Barrikady" plant. This article so enraged Vareykis, that he dismissed me from my job and defamed me publicly (see "Stalingrad Pravda" for 12.1.1936). Only after pressure from the public (a letter from the plant's workers to "Pravda") was I four months later rehabilitated as a feuilletonist to be able to publish. And in 1937 in the Stalingrad department of NKVD I was informed that Budnyak had been executed by shooting, and my feuilleton was attached to his file as part of the evidence against him.

3) In the autumn of 1937 "Tikhookeanskaya Zvezda" published my feuilleton entitled "Under the Signboard of Musical Comedy" which uncovered a group of the anti-Soviet minded in the Khabarovsk theatre. The group fell victim to repression.

This is only what I can now recall. In general, "Kommuna" and "Stalingradskaya Pravda" printed 8-10 of my articles every months in which I impartially and poignantly came down on the facts of anti-Soviet and anti-Party character. A number of these articles and feuilletons, on one hand, as you see, proved to be of help to the organs. On the other hand (as is becoming clear now), they remained a sty in Vareykis's eye. This is why it is not at all surprising that during the inquiry in 1937, overwhelmed by the hatred to each and all who but brushed him with their little finger directly or indirectly, Vareykis called out my name, attempting to also strike a blow at me.

In addition, I consider it my duty to inform you that working in Stalingrad, I was for many years a secret collaborator for the organs. And no one forced then me to do this work: I did of my own good will because I always thought it my duty, as I do now, to continually help the organs in unmasking the enemies of the USSR in any situation. This I did and go on doing...

Carrying out concrete tasks from the organs, I submitted to the Stalingrad NKVD department a number of materials about the anti-Soviet agitation waged by separate individuals and groups of people employed in the fields of art and literature. In particular, these materials contained information about slanderous works of local writers G. Smolyakov, I. Vladsky and others (convicted by the organs); about the systematic agitation for the enemy carried out by the Finnish subject and artist of the Stalingrad Drama Theatre G. I. Gorelov (a.k.a. G. I. Polezhayev), who disguised this activity by simulating mental infirmity (convicted in 1941); about inimical discreditation of the famous Soviet writer A. N. Tolstoy by F. I. Terentyev at the banquet given at the editorial office in 1936, etc...

On the 29th May 1950 I submitted a statement to the USSR Ministry of State Security (via investigator Chumakov) concerning subversive activities of a number of people employed in the Soviet film industry. Judging from the newspapers, some of my information was confirmed and all of them were executed...

In December of 1950 in the Ozerlag camp unit no. 2, I handed the authorities a written pledge to collaborate with them in unmasking persons carrying on anti-Soviet agitation. This collaboration I render sincerely and honestly; and I experience moral satisfaction from knowing that even here in the unusual circumstances I make a certain contribution toward the common cause of fighting the enemies of the USSR.

...Of course, I am not a saint. There were mistakes in my life. But these were unintentional and accidental, never harmful to the common cause. Such is my life and such is my work. And such is their cruel end.

I appeal to you as to the member of the Soviet government, as to the Minister of the State Security:

do not leave this letter without attention;

do not allow that my life and my creative abilities be lost in vain for I can, want and must bring an even greater use;

please order that my case be reviewed taking into account all that was stated here; lift the heavy burden of slander away from me; show me your political trust and I will justify it in every way.

Boris Dyakov
7th January 1952
Ozerlag Camp, Unit 02

If anyone of our readers wishes to know more about "secret collaborators," they can write to the author of the above-cited letter. Here is his address and telephone number:

Boris Dyakov
USSR, Moscow 129010
Astrakhansky per., 5, kv. 38
Telephone: 280-08-90

GREAT MASTERS OF FALSIFICATION:

One of the tasks of the Soviet secret police was to doctor official photographs after each purge. Bottom photo shows Stalin with Frunze, Voroshilov and Ordzhonikidze, after more than half of the group above have been executed. If one looks closely, one can recognise the fake.

Section III

CONDUCTING INTERNAL INTELLIGENCE

The conduct of internal intelligence and its development are not subject to fixed patterns. They demand, amongst other things, adaptation to local conditions and circumstances, constant comparison of all data and current instructions of the investigatory organ, development of initiative and ability to make correct deductions and also to correct opportunely one's own and collaborators'.

On starting as an investigator one often meets collaborators who have considerably more experience of the anti-Soviet movement, with people of highly developed will. Therefore, it is necessary to establish oneself definitely amongst collaborators and work out methods to use in discussion with collaborators and in the direction of their work.

At the start of investigatory activity one should allow collaborators to express themselves more and answer definite questions exclusively directed at definition of anti-Soviet activity of an organisation and persons connected with it.

Explaining methods of conspiracy to a collaborator, one should in no way ever acquaint him with the organisation of the Intelligence Bureau and its members, always bearing in mind that relations with a collaborator are just temporary and that many of them can let one down at any time.

One should especially beware of a collaborator's influence upon one and his exploitation. Although one should maintain close and delicate relations with a collaborator, one's demands as to the communication of investigatory material and intolerance of provocation must be absolute.

One should be wary of collaborator's giving information of a general character and just to do with the past activity of the organisation. If the collaborator is not convinced as to the criminal activity of persons still at liberty he is, consequently, still insufficiently inclined to work in the investigatory organ.

One must relate warily to persons who have served earlier in other intelligence bureaux. One should always make inquiries about these persons, even despite their persuasive requests, in the places of their former employ. Often the mentioned persons, already compromised in investigation, give fictitious information about nonexistent groups and subsequently put those in charge of the investigation in a vcry awkward position. In order to determine how far a collaborator is actually acquainted with the anti-Soviet environment, one should obtain answers from him to the following questions:

1) In what do the main principles of the organisation about which he is giving information consist (collaborators introduced into an organisation for investigation can be acquainted with its character)?
2) What literature was and is being distributed?
3) What arrests have been carried out in this organisation and which of its members were at liberty?
4) How informed is the local organisation and of which sections does it consist?

And other questions which would convince one that the person is actually acquainted with local or other work.

The intelligence received from the collaborator must be immediately checked and external surveillances developed. Besides, on checking roundabout questions should be given, inquiries about the activity of the establishment made, etc.

One should make an especially thorough check when starting to work with a collaborator, as many of them will lie and exaggerate from the beginning.

Starting to work with a collaborator the following should be unfailingly instilled in him:

1. Neither the militia nor anybody except the head of the Agency should know that he works for investigation: this should be in no case revealed: neither when detained by members of the militia, the frontier guard, etc.

2. That the collaborator may in no case enter the establishment conducting the investigation, which always entails discovery as these establishments are under surveillance by anti-Soviet groups.

3. That giving information the collaborator should indicate exactly:

a) The source it was obtained from.
b) What he personally heard, read in newspapers, proclamations and other illegal and anti-Soviet literature.
c) Of what he has been witness, what he knows through rumour or unconfirmed rumour.

4. That he should bring to interviews literature he has received as well as all letters, stamps and documents entrusted to him for safekeeping by enemies of the people. After they were made use of, the latter items

should be immediately returned to the collaborator and so quickly that their removal should not reflect on his reputation in the organisation.

5. That the collaborator is absolutely forbidden to disguise himself, wear make-up, follow, question or treat his comrades with the aim of investigation; or to improve his living conditions by the acquisition of any things, including clothes and small items, with money obtained from the investigatory organ. Seen from outside, it is desirable that the collaborator consider himself, with rare exceptions, a needy person.

6. That he, being present in an anti-Soviet environment to pursecute it in the course of the law, cannot himself commit crimes and incite the people around. His role should be as secret as possible, and as far as possible consist of intermediary work or acting out orders, so that even if he is arrested, he could not be found guilty of anti-Sovict work.

7. That any falsehood and provocation, even if it is of slight degree, entails not only a cessation of their work for the investigation department, but that besides the collaborator answers for it with all severitiy, up to execution.

8. That a collaborator has no right to keep any forbidden objects (bombs, literature, firearms etc.) without the knowledge of the one in charge of the investigation.

9. Frequent meetings and lengthy interviews should be held with collaborators (but not to the detriment of secrecy). Experience has shown that the collaborator knows considerably more than he says of his own initiative and that due to superficial conversations and infrequent meetings very serious matters may be missed.

Meetings with collaborators ought to be arranged with the greatest secrecy, preventing the possibility of one collaborator running into another. Besides which it is necessary to put the collaborator in such a position that he can always communicate information but not be suspected of culpable absence. For this he should have a private address for letters and the possibility of meeting in the street. Ordinarily the route by which an employee goes to and from work is indicated. A collaborator having something urgent to communicate goes past the employee and throws a cigarette into an empty matchbox after lighting it. The employee picks it up and hands with a note to the head agent. Such meetings can take place in intercommunicating houses, on staircases etc.

For the surveillance of conspiracy no trifle should be ignored, as absent-mindedness and negligence very often leads to slip-ups.

When a meeting takes place at a secret flat the door should always be kept locked. Clothes, shawls, galoshes, canes and other objects belonging to the collaborator should not be left in the passage. The collaborator should not be sat opposite a mirror or windows. When leaving the flat, the one who has been speaking with the collaborator should go out first to avoid a chance encounter.

From time to time a watch should be kept by experienced and trustworthy people over the secret flat to ascertain that the flat is being vacated or to see who is coming into the house.

Special attention should be paid to the method of carrying on secret intelligence which we will repeat as an exercise.

All intelligence received from secret collaborators should be documented exactly, since repetition of the surveillance will delay the investigation.

When making arrests one should strive toward two aims: 1) to disorganise and break the anti-Soviet organisation, and 2) not to block the work of the informer and give him a possibility to work.

One sometimes has to arrest collaborators to warn them of something. But this should be resorted to only in extreme circumstances as it cannot be repeated.

If a collaborator has been arrested, one should take measures that his release should not serve as the cause of his discovery. For this reason several persons of his group together with the collaborator are freed at the same time so that he can take his place in the organisation.

The collaborator must be given a special name for secrecy, similar to his family name, patronymic or characteristic quality: under this nickname, or "pseudonym," he registers with intelligence.

MAIN QUESTIONS TO WHICH A COLLABORATOR SHOULD ALWAYS HAVE READY ANSWERS

1. Which of the more active members is known to him at the given moment and how and where can he be taken into surveillance?

2. What information does he have about all the politically unreliable persons he comes in contact with? For which purpose one should inquire about everything known

about the person's past and present activity, and not only in relation to work but also family affairs.

3. The structure of the organisation or group from top to bottom.

4. Literature such as dissident and samizdat periodicals and magazines, anti-Soviet works, as well as censored publications likewise distributed with the aim of propaganda. Publications should be brought in by collaborators whenever possible.

> ***Samizdat*** *means "self-publishing." Materials that cannot be published by official organisations are published, printed, multiplied and distributed anonymously and are known as "samizdat" publications.*

5. Of what does the active work at the moment consist?

6. What immediate forms will the dissident activity of separate persons and groups take? Special attention must be paid to prepared demonstrations and other events which should be anticipated in good time and disorganised.

7. Who went, who came, with what aim, where and for what period of time and with what connections?

8. What is known about stores and storage of arms etc.?

9. What is known about the activity of other dissident groups and people belonging to them?

10. Questions about the degree of the organisation's development at the given moment and other relevant questions, dependent on the circumstances of the case.

11. What are the mood and the aims of the associate anti-Soviet organisations in outlying districts? What is the attitude of the nationalist movements to anti-Soviet activities and goals?

12. To what organisation was the collaborator affiliated?

The copy is verified against the original.
Secretary.

* * *

SCENE FROM EVERY-DAY LIFE
IN A FORCED-LABOUR CAMP

A drawing by an inmate. A criminal prisoner is "educating" a political prisoner, "the enemy of the people," whose life in the camp was not worth more than that of a fly. The KGB guards approve heartily.

INSTRUCTION TO INVESTIGATORS OF KGB FOR FIGHTING ANTI-SOVIET ACTIVITIES AND PROFITEERING

produced at the General Conference of KGB
25th March 1989

1. The investigator receives the file with the following data:

   1) Reports from the secret section (from intelligence or undercover agents).
   2) Search warrant.
   3) Protocol of search or audit.
   4) Material evidence removed during search, etc.

2. The investigator gets thoroughly acquainted with all the materials handed to him, after which he proceeds to the interrogation of the accused, witnesses and informants.

3. Before anything else the following statistical information is entered in the protocol:

   1) Family name, name, patronymic, address, date of birth (age)
   2) Former names, registered place of residence
   3) Information on parents
   4) Profession or trade
   5) Place of education
   6) Whether the person was tried before in court
   7) Military service record

Note. Depending on the importance of the case, the above information can be expanded or abbreviated.

4. Then questions are put in systematic order to which

an immediate, accurate and clear answer is demanded from the accused.

5. When interrogating signs of torture should not be evident; the interrogator should not shout at the accused, should not to get angry, but instead be restrained, polite, correct and, above all, observant.

Any interrogator that would behave himself correctly would not last on his job more than a day. But Soviet people understand very well that appeals for the struggle for peace really mean appeals for armament. 'Liberation' of Baltic states really meant enslavement of free countries by the totalitarian state. And 'liberation' of the Soviet peasantry means their lifetime attachment to the village where they were born (a return to serfdom). Etc.

About the 'correctness' of KGB interrogators one could judge from the statements of the people well versed in this subject. During the past fifteen years in the languages of the Soviet Union a new expression appeared: "press-camera" (press-cell) or "press-khata" (press-cabin). In translation this means a room where pressure is exerted on a prisoner. For this reason a newly arrested person is placed in a cell with two or three criminals who had agreed to collaborate with the prison administration and beat up the newcomer in exchange for various privileges. Here are some statements (mainly by prisoners) from which one can judge the "correctness" of the system's interrogators.

"In the old wing there are twelve cells in the basement. There is also a basement annexe with cells number 122 through 127. These are used for torturing prisoners. There they are beaten up to death, constrained by handcuffs and straight jackets... Deputy prison governor in charge of the regime Umarkulov directs tortures and murders...

The day I was taken to the Andizhan prison, I was called in by Umarkulov and head of the special section Azimov. They started to hound me, threaten with physical violence... Later I was convinced that there are really such cells here, with the criminals, their executors. Administration puts people in these cells for any transgressions. There they are beaten up to death and raped. They do everything that one can think of. In the same prison there is a place where the wardens take the inmates and beat them up to death." (From Samizdat publication No. 3723, Concerning the situation in the Andizhan prison, P.O.Box 64, ST-1, Andizhan, Uzbek Republic)

After an escape by four inmates from this prison, the guards attacked a prisoner nicknamed "Boxer":

"..I personally saw the whole reprisal with this victim. This happened in January, beginning of February of 1977... Azimov and Umarkulov were present at the murder. He was not killed right away — the tortures lasted for four days. After the murder the doctors performed an autopsy right in the cell no. 137. The prisoners from the cells nos. 138 and 139 saw this."

Writer Georgy Vladimov, a former chairman of the Soviet section of Amnesty International, informs:

"Also in fashion today are the press-cameras. The accused are put in cells together with usually two criminals who beat them up, as with Alexey Smirnov-Kosterin. Rape also happens. And each time the investigator calls the accused and asks: "So, shall we sign?"

Former inmates of the Tbilisi prison Tsirekidze and Usupyan occupied the same cell in 1970-73 with persons under investigation whom they beat up on orders from KGB. In this way they "solved" over 200 "crimes." Upon their release from the prison Tsirekidze wrote that the whole second wing of the Tbilisi high security prison no. 1 was "special. In its every cell there were agents placed and who worked with the objects according to special assignments, for which they were given drugs, alcohol, meetings with relatives, right to receive parcels, promised to be freed, etc."

Tsirekidze worked in the cell no. 40, where among his "objects" were Karlo Tsupaya, arrested 30th March 1973 and sentenced for 10 years "for accepting a bribe." Tsupaya's friends released a leaflet in which Tsupaya stated that he was beaten up unconscious from the very first day and that the doctors had to be called to help him come to.

"I was pierced with iron rods, hit with a chair on the head; they put out cigarettes on my arms and promised to kill me if I did not sign the statements incriminating myself."

Tsupaya also attests:

"Murderer Tsirekidze before my very eyes tortured another prisoner Michitashvili and even committed with him the act of sodomy in various refined ways. Half-alive, he was taken to hospital in May of 1973 and I have not seen him since."

In the years of perestroika Tsirekidze himself said:

"I also worked over object Harshivala for which I got an assignment from Shavishvili and Esakiya to 'sodomise' him because being a future acknowledged criminal, he had to be "corrupted."

Here one ought to note that according to the custom of the inmates of Soviet camps, the man who played a passive role in a homosexual encounter even if it were once and against his will, becomes a pariah. Other inmates do not admit him into their midst and he is given the most dirty and humiliating tasks, including prostituting himself to other prisoners.

"There were cases when after a serious beating prisoners died in hospitals which "wrote them off," i.e. false diagnoses were concocted and death was attributed to various diseases."

All of the above-cited is taken from the file of documents collected by today's president of Georgia Zviyad Gamsakhurdiya.

The same took place on all of the territory of the Soviet Union until 1991. According to the statements of Ivan Kovalyov, member of the Moscow Group for Promoting of Observance of Helsinki Agreements, Sirvard Avagyan stayed in the women's colony UK-272/11 in the Irkutsk Region, for over half a year and every day she was beaten up by the inmates under the leadership of the deputy head of political work Uvarova and the head of the detachment Galina Fritsuk. From the first day of her stay she was beaten up till she bled. For several days she was not given anything to eat.

"She was beaten up by men, members of the camp staff, by women inmates. Five to eight people took part in beatings. They used their hands and feet. Until she foamed at the mouth, vomited, lost consciousness. Sirvard was released from the camp barely alive, blackened, having lost 32 kilos."

It is possible that Avagyan simply was not to the liking of the sadists Uvarova and Fritsuk from the first sight.

Locksmith Mikhail Kukobaka (born in 1936) from Bobruysk, Belorussia, was put in prison for offering a Western radio station his article about human rights in Russia. On 13th August 1982 he was sentenced to imprisonment. He writes about his experience in the Yelets prison (Lipetsk Region, RSFSR):

"Everything that goes on in this prison is long

known to the Republican Department of Prisons. And if this is not enough, most likely they unofficially inspire all the abuses. A certain "Vologodsky method" is used when the most hardened criminals are given a completely free hand in the cells with the purpose of "re-education" of the others and over-fulfilment of the plan in work. Occurrences of sodomy by rape are commonplace. Many left the prison physical and mental invalids. There were cases of direct murder. However, everything was "written off" and none was held responsible."

About the same situation with rape of prisoners in the Leningrad prison in the 1980's writes philologist and Germanic scholar Konstantin A. Zadovsky. About the same situation in Moscow prison writes Alexey Smirnov, etc., etc.

6. Do not miss one movement, one frown, one glance of the accused, for by observing each gesture the investigator can acquire much irrefutable data.

7. Do not permit one superfluous word or lofty phrase. Only in a case where there is no data, no lead on which to question the accused, allow the accused to tell all that has "happened" in order from that to conclude what the truth of the matter and accusation is.

8. Give questions which are strictly thought out; but in no way let the accused into those facts which are already known.

9. Dependent on the accused, sometimes give questions quickly, boldly, decisively; write down all answers; give contradictory questions in order then, when the accused gives different answers, by way of logical deduction to conclude contradiction in answers, and thus to confuse

the accused and insist firmly on confession and exact answers.

10. Pay attention to the surroundings during questioning and the mood of the accused, for the immediate surroundings have an immediate effect on the most resolute person.

11. If several persons are involved in a case question them all, and then proceed to the interrogation of essential witnesses.

12. If during questioning other facts are revealed, like the involvement of other persons, give immediate instructions through the necessary organs about revisions, searches, arrests etc.

13. If necessary arrange confrontations with witnesses, and during these confrontations bear strictly in mind:

a) Do not allow one word to be uttered before the investigator has given a question to one or the other side.
b) Observe the slightest movement of both sides.
c) On giving questions to one side observe the actions of the other side.

14. When conducting an interrogation, present material evidence so that the accused gives an explanation.

Note. Especially bear in mind that one should not present unnecessary material evidence but only such that would incline the accused to a confession.

15. After preliminary questioning but not later than 3 days after receipt, the investigator composes a resolution (either in his name or in the name of the section or

committee) about the measure of restraint and a charge is presented.

Measures of restraint can be:

a) Seizure of documents.
b) Signed statement not to leave town and to appear.
c) Surveillance.
d) Bail.
e) Pledge.
f) Imprisonment.

Note. The charge is presented in written form. The accused should sign that he has received it.

16. In the course of 14 days the investigator investigates the case, questions all persons involved, examining records, papers and material evidence, giving orders about further searches, etc.

17. Not later than 15 days after the investigator has received the case, a decision has to be drawn up in which the origin of the case, the results of the investigation and the degree of guilt of each accused must be detailed, based on the existing resolutions of the Soviet authorities, the provisioning organs, the Council of Ministers, etc.

Note. If for important reasons the investigator has no possibility of concluding the case in 15 days, he appeals with motivated applications through the President of the Investigatory Collegium to the Presidium attached to the Committee, and the term of the investigation can be prolonged only with the permission of the Department.

18. The investigator reports concluded cases at the general meeting of the Department or Committee for classification of the resolution.

ON INVESTIGATORY COLLEGIA

1) An investigatory collegium is formed from investigators and investigators' assistants, and sometimes from inspectors.

2) An investigatory collegium is a collective institution, but only investigators have the right of the deciding voice.

3) An investigatory collegium is formed in the aim of perfecting the internal order of investigatory work and acquainting all new investigators, assistant investigators and inspectors with their duties.

4) An investigatory collegium in all its work is subordinate to the corresponding Department or the KGB.

5) The investigatory collegium elects from its own midst a president, vice president and secretary.

6) The president of the investigatory collegium can issue orders to the apparatus; i.e he assigns cases, follows progress of the investigation, observes whether the investigation is proceeding legally, etc.

7) The president of the investigatory collegium can issue orders only of an internal organisational character and is, as are the investigators in all their work, subordinate to the Department and KGB.

RULES FOR CONDUCTING AN INQUIRY

1. The Special Committee for anti-Soviet and economic crimes does not conduct full investigations but only a preliminary inquiry.

Note. If the importance of a case warrants an investigation and not an inquiry, this is done by resolution of the Presidium of the Committee or Department.

2. The question of an inquiry is instituted by individual members or departments and also by instruction of the organs of the Central Authority. Where a lapse of Soviet authority is concerned, an investigation can be replaced by an inquiry.

3. The aim of a preliminary inquiry is the exposure of an important State crime. The tasks of the Special Committees, Communications Officers, Regional and District Departments are wider.

4. Committing a State crime entails conspiracy of a whole number of persons who have previously plotted together. If a leaflet has been found in X's house criticising the Soviet authority, questions must arise. Where did he get it? Who printed it? Concerning where it was printed, one must look deeper, find out what sort of organisation it was whose ideas X took up. When conducting inquiries in such cases, the material seized during the search is important in the form of letters, notes, manuscripts, notebooks, writing pads, etc.

5. When conducting an inquiry of the Special Committee, the ranks of the local militia should offer all assistance.

6. Copies are taken from important inquiries and sent to the KGB.

7. When inquiries are made on military personnel, the Ministry of Defence is informed.

8. An inquiry is instituted when there are sufficient grounds, e.g. slanderous letters, popular rumours, etc.

9. The militia leaves everything in its place and allows no one to the scene of the crime until the arrival of the legal authorities.

10. If a criminal action has been committed in several provinces, the inquiry is carried out by one of the Regional Committees by proposal of the KGB.

11. In liquidating a conspiracy, the Bureau of Investigation draws up a record of liquidation which it hands to the corresponding Department.

12. The investigator who has received a record of liquidation from the Bureau of Investigation, consults with the head of Department as to how best to conduct the inquiry.

13. If it is necessary to liquidate a large conspiracy quickly, one must draw up a detailed memorandum of who is involved, make a plan of action, and only then proceed to the liquidation.

14. An inquiry is instituted in the following circumstances:
a) a plot against Soviet authority,
b) an insult to Soviet authority in the person of the supreme organs,
c) incitement of the population against Soviet authority,

d) instigation again Soviet authority,
e) abuse of the name of one of the Soviet institutions without being connected with it,
f) incitement to anti-Soviet violence,
g) kindling of national divisions,
h) open call to nonfulfilment of the orders of the state institutions and to secret opposition to Soviet orders and secret sabotage,
i) monarchist anti-Soviet agitation or dissident activity,
j) literature inciting acts of violence or criticising Soviet form of government,
k) premeditated and harmful correspondence.

If evidence is inconclusive a preliminary secret surveillance should be instituted.

15. During an inquiry the investigating authorities have the right to investigate people in high positions.

16. One must aim to gather as much information about the guilty as possible.

17. To incline the accused to confession is a difficult matter and demands great agility and skill from the person conducting the inquiry. In the Middle Ages inquisitional method permitted torture. Now that type of torture is not permitted. Officials should show every assistance during an inquiry.

How those confessions were extracted from innocent people the world learnt from a speech made by Khrushchev at the 20th Party Congress of the Soviet Communist Party in Kremlin on 25th February 1956.

Nikita Sergeyevich Khrushchev, the first secretary of Communist Party and premier of the Soviet Union, said:

"When the files of some of these so-called 'spies' and 'saboteurs' were examined, it was found that all their cases were fabricated. Confessions of guilt made by many of those arrested and charged with hostile activity were obtained by means of cruel and inhuman tortures."

Of the case of Robert Eikhe, who was an alternate member of the Politburo until his arrest in 1938, Khrushchev said:

"Eikhe was forced under torture to sign in advance a statement containing his confession drawn up by the investigating judges, in which he and several other eminent Party workers were accused of anti-Soviet activity."

Khrushchev also quoted from a statement which Eikhe sent to Stalin six months after his arrest in which he said:

"Not being able to suffer the tortures to which I was subjected by Ushakov and Nikolayev — and especially by the former — who took advantage of the fact that my broken ribs had not properly mended and were causing me great pain, I was forced to incriminate myself and others."

Khrushchev also quoted from Eikhe's statement on the eve of his execution, in which he said:

"In all the so-called confessions of mine there is not a single letter written by me with the exception of my signatures at the bottom of the statements, which were forced from me. I made my confession under pressure by the investigating judge who tortured me from the time of my arrest."

Khrushchev himself asked the question that had been asked in the West at the time the "confessions" were being made:

"How is it possible that a person confesses to

crimes which he has not committed? Only in one way — because of the application of methods involving physical pressure on him, torturing him and reducing him to a state of unconsciousness, depriving him of his judgement and destroying his dignity as a human being. This is the way the 'confessions' were obtained."

To cap it all, Mr. Khrushchev quoted the text of a telegram which Stalin sent to party officials in defence of the methods being used by the police. It said:

"The Central Committee of the All-Union Communist Party explains that the application of methods of physical pressure in NKVD (secret police) practice is permissible from 1937 onwards..."

Finally, Khrushchev described Stalin's advice to the police in the purges he initiated shortly before his death in 1953:

"Stalin personally called the investigating judge, gave him instructions and advised him which methods of investigation to use: these methods were simple — beat, beat and beat again."

Thus Mr. Khrushchev answered the question which had puzzled the world for so long. The simple answer was: "Beat, beat and beat again."

For daring to criticise KGB, a few years later a plot was hatched and Khrushchev lost his job.

18. Witnesses should not be given questions which they do not understand. Evidence should be presented as things took place and not as the witness perceived them. It is necessary that the witness give facts but not be permitted lofty phrases. Witnesses are called directly to the cell.

19. Inquiry of the accused begins with presenting the accusation laid against him. At the inquiry one should clarify that one is dealing with the right person.

20. First the protocol is written, then statistical information, the questions which are given to the accused after the first inquiry; then the question of imprisonment or release is decided. If the accused had refused to give evidence then this is noted in the protocol. While the inquiry is being conducted, each item of material evidence must be presented so that the accused can explain each.

21. On an inquiry into anti-Soviet cases one must rely on material evidence and not on the evidence of the accused.

22. It is necessary, without resorting to torture, to extract as much as possible from the accused. Here all must be done and it all depends on the skill of the person conducting the inquiry. In conducting an inquiry one must pay attention to the surroundings as these are sometimes conducive to frank confession. Then the accused must be convinced by the inquirer that he is harming the state. Things should be done so as not immediately to show one's cards to the accused, but gradually reveal what the person conducting the inquiry knows. The protocol should be clear and complete.

23. The person conducting the inquiry first goes through a definite system of questions; then he asks the accused to write them down or does so himself. Information about each accused is communicated to the Registration Bureau of the Committee. The bureau is also asked whether they have material about the accused. If the defendant is a soldier, the Military Department of the district is approached.

24. Measures of restraint for evasion of an inquiry can be:

1) seizure of documents
2) signed statement not to leave town and to attend the inquiry
3) militia surveillance
4) release on bail
5) taking of a pledge
6) taking under guard

25. In each separate case a resolution of the Committee, Presidium of the Department or head of the Department is made at their discretion. An inquiry is made about persons sought and hiding, and information is gathered in the KGB. For searching in provinces, inquiries should be directed to KGB; it sends out search posters.

26. Searches at houses of persons against whom there are definite instructions should be conducted straight away. Searches are resorted to when no evidence can be obtained about a given person in any other way.

27. Answerability for their evidence should be pointed out to witnesses, and false evidence ought not to be given out of friendship or hostility.Sometimes confrontations are arranged for witnesses to clear up contradictions.

28. Everything seized is entered in the protocol. Then detainees are questioned about the articles seized, while they are watched for what they are going to say. Material evidence is sorted into packets, a list of the items is composed and then a resolution is made.

29. Using all methods to clarify active or subjective truth, the person conducting the inquiry should aim to get possession of evidence that would say that such and such a crime has been committed, or such and such a person should be brought before an inquiry. A resolution

is made to conduct an inquiry where the motives for the inquiry are proved. If an inquiry is conducted about many persons, one resolution is not sufficient for all.

30. An inquiry concludes dependent on the essence of the matter, material etc. The question of the concluding of an inquiry is decided by the investigators and the head of the Department.

31. After which further direction of the case is decided, whether it is transferred or concluded. All material evidence etc. is attached to the case.

32. Each Committee, Centre or Department should keep a list of arrested and suspected persons, a record of the number of inquiries, and copies of the papers for each case.

33. When an inquiry is begun, information about this is sent to the KGB.

34. All Committees should present on a yearly basis reports on inquiries which they have been conducting to the KGB headquarters.

TORTURES USED BY SOVIET SECRET POLICE IN ALL ITS INSTITUTIONS

Drawings and text by an inmate.
1) fist for smashing face and squeezing testicles; 2) rubber hose and truncheons for beating; 3) belt for strangling; 4) feet in boots for massaging ribs, stomach, back and other parts of the body; 5) small sack with sand or an iron in a felt boot for beating (not to leave traces); 6) rubber or plastic bag for "cutting oxygen;" 7) barbiturates; 8) hanging "rack;" 9) bottle for insertion in vagina or anus; 10) victim with bear buttocks is seated on a chamber-pot with a rat in it, and then the vessel is heated from below using a hot-plate.

RULES OF CONSPIRACY FOR FREEDOM FIGHTERS

We want to look albeit in the most superficial way into the sphere of secret practice and note the most important of those blunders which frequently occur, partly through negligence, partly through ignorance.

SECRET FLAT

Flat

1. On hiring a flat, albeit just for accomodation, it is always necessary to pay attention to: how isolated it is from neighbours, whether the walls are thick, whether there are internal doors, onto where the windows look out. The windows of one comrade's flat looked onto a tall hill and spies used to climb onto the slope in the evening and observed through the window what was going on in the room with the greatest of ease. Naturally, assessment of this flat from this viewpoint should be made intelligently and diplomatically in order not to awake the owner's suspicion. Special attention and thought must be shown when hiring a flat for special purposes: for meetings, a printing press etc.

2. In countries where identity card registration is required, like West Germany, the identity card should only be registered when it is no longer possible to delay or avoid it. Any superfluous registration mark on the identity card is always inconvenient. Again here one should not awaken any suspicion on the part of the owners and caretakers.

3. Always bear in mind that many owners of furnished rooms and a quite significant percentage of caretakers can show favours to the intelligence agents. This is practised in particular in university towns.

4. Two or more comrades should not live in one flat: failure of one reflects in one way or another on the other mates. To a certain degree it is permissible to live together with a law-abiding resident. But one must bear in mind that in the case of arrest your fellow tenant will be questioned as witness and, of course, he can do much damage by his simple-hearted and frank evidence.

5. Whatever trust we may feel towards our servants, landlords or neighbours, one must always bear in mind that in the case of our arrest they will be questioned, shown photographs, inquiries after, etc. We are not talking of those cases when they may betray us unintentionally, through their naívete. Therefore, all measures should be taken that the staff see visitors as little as possible and nothing be known of the secret work of the tenant.

6. It is best of all to arrange for the flat to be locked when the occupants are out, and that the whereabouts of the key be known to one or two comrades. This makes it possible for the latter in case of sudden arrest (in the street, at a meeting, station etc.) to clear the flat immediately of any compromising material.

7. If you engage in illegal work at home you should not forget to keep doors locked to prevent the flat being visited by strangers.

8. It is absolutely necessary to arrange a set of signals in

the event of arrest. It is also not a bad idea to signal to show whether we're in or not: this saves us from useless visits to one another. It could be said that we should have a good signalling system in our flats and its absence often brings about quite unecessary sacrifices. Signals should be of such a type that outsiders could not guess them as a signal could be faked.

9. One should frequently search one's flat for incriminating papers, tapes etc. which could be found at search.

10. Do not store various materials, like printing inks, offset plates, toners and similar things in one's flat.

11. Leaving one's flat, we should not give to such comrades as visited us earlier and were noticed by the owners, for this establishes a clear link between them and us. If we want to give it to somebody, it is necessary that he rent the room independently as if from an advertisement.

12. Our lifestyle, our appearance, dress etc. should be such as to be as little strange as possible.

13. In one's secret flat lifestyle should be thought out and restrained in the highest degree. One should not stay up at nights, sing illegal songs, make suspicious noise or live too much to oneself. It is necessary to carry on a lifestyle which fits one's declared profession. Failures frequently come from the least expected quarters. In one place the tenants awoke the landlord's suspicion that they were engaged in forging money.

14. Those living at a secret flat should endeavour to be seen as little as possible by those they should avoid; so that in the event of one of them being arrested outside their home, his residence could not be immediately established.

15. With this aim of saving the secret flat in the event of arrest outside, residents should not carry with them identity cards showing their residence as also their other documents, visiting cards etc. which establish their identity.

16. Work accompanied with noise should not be carried out at night.

17. More than anything one's flat should be guarded from the visitation of spies. At their first appearance one's address should be changed as quickly and carefully as possible.

In the Street

18. Leaving the house, one should always bear in mind the possibility of sudden arrest in the street. Therefore do not carry anything compromising unnecessarily.

19. Always bear spies in mind but behave wisely: do not cast anxious looks, do not be rude or demonstrative. Make sure in other ways: by travelling by communicating courtyards and deserted side streets, by jumping on moving buses etc.

20. The tactics of spies are extremely well worked out and varied. Very often, for example, they pass the "game" for which they hunt from hand to hand, from block to block, going by parallel streets, running ahead etc. Therefore, if for the whole way we have not noticed a single figure following us from beginning to end, if suspicious persons that attract our attention disappear without following us — this still does not prove anything. If we have to visit the

secret flat often then, although we have managed to cover our tracks on the way and lose the spies, nevertheless they will be every time closer to the goal. For they will be lying in wait in the place where they lost us the last time, thanks to which they will soon get to the secret flat. It is necessary to always bear this in mind and scrupulously check one's movements both at the start and end of the way. In important cases when it is necessary to go to the secret address and we do not trust our own surveillance, we should entrust an experienced and uncompromised comrade to follow behind us at a reasonable distance and make sure that we are not being followed.

21 Spies frequently work as cabbies, shopkeepers, hot dog and ice-cream peddlers, etc.

22 In no case should one go down the street in pairs and, even worse, in groups. Likewise one should not appear together in social places, theatres and parks. Nor should one arrange business meetings in the street, squares, restaurants.

23. Do not carry open packets, even at night.

24. One should avoid large stations by every possible means, and also be careful in the post office.

25. On meeting comrades in the street never exchange greetings.

26. Approaching one's house, one should not tell one's cabbie to stop right by one's flat.

27. Comrades! One should not entrust short-sighted individuals with functions where one is liable to encounter spies. Their assurances that they are not being followed or that everything is alright should be regarded with

scepticism.

28 As soon as it is ascertained that someone is being followed, he must be immediately and decisively isolated, putting all other considerations aside. Anyone who out of a commendable zeal for work hides from comrades or plays down the fact of being followed is committing a crime.

29. The organisation should from time to time arrange its own surveillance of its members to ensure that they are being secretive enough and that spies are not following them.

30. One should not stop for the night in a suspicious place that is being watched. In Chile four persons visited a worker to spend the night with him. They discovered him burning certain literature as he was expecting a search. The guests calmed him and stayed to pass the night. In the same night all five were arrested from this flat.

31. One should not see off the departing.

32. Comrades should not make social visits to one another.

33. When calling on a comrade, arranged signals should be carefully observed and attention should be paid to suspicious particulars. Care should be doubled on visiting flats in a strange town when passing through.

34. Visiting a comrade and not having found him at home, one should not leave him illegal notes or things on the table or in any other place. Such lapses have often led to fateful consequences. In Germany one person received through someone a coded letter. He carried it to the

addressee and not finding him at home (he was living in furnished rooms), wrote a "legal" note, where he gave to understand to look under the tablecloth, and left it on the table. Next day, getting uneasy, he visited the addressee again. It turned out that the latter had read the note but did not understand it, and the letter was still under the tablecloth. On that same night quite unexpectedly a search was made at the addressee's residence, but, of course, nothing was found. The letter was of such a nature that if it had been found, the writer and his intermediaries would have been discovered.

35. One should exercise utmost care with an unknown individual from different parts, even though he comes to the secret address with an agreed password. At first he should be just questioned and told nothing, his communications compared the lack of contradictions in his story established, etc.

36. To cut out mutual visits, one could sometimes use telephones (extremely carefully) or the town postal and parcel service, observing, of course, the necessary precautions.

37. Members of the organization should be known by nicknames, fictitious first names and family names. The actual family name should be unknown. But one should bear in mind that when in "society" some individual, unlike the others, becomes known by a nickname, it attracts attention to him and can have nasty consequences. One should also not be known under the family name of his false identity card.

38. One should not have one's genuine initials on one's belongings. This often gives traitors a clue to seek out individuals whose family names they know.

Gatherings

39. One cannot arrange meetings, even small, in flats where literature or other illegal things are stored.

40. In a flat where a committee or other analogous body is sitting, there should not be any objects which would indicate the presence of a meeting and its activity, like the committee's stamp, letters etc. Objects which are always necessary should be sited where they can quickly be destroyed (e.g. in front of a burning fire).

41. Departing for a large meeting, illegal evening, demonstration, festival, or generally any place where there are chances of being arrested, one should carefully clean one's flat up, examine wastepaper baskets, lock doors so that no comrade could enter and be there accidentally during a search.

Travel

42. The most dangerous point on a journey is the railway station, bus terminal or airport, and the procedure of buying a ticket is particularly dangerous. One must be extremely careful here.

43. The ticket should be to somewhat further than the point you are travelling to, so that if arrested en route, the end point of the journey cannot be found out from the ticket.

44. In especially important cases one should stop in some intermediate point to check whether one has a "tail," and, accordingly, to change the route, to continue by foot or some alternative means of transport, etc.

45. Travelling to an important secret meeting, in the time just before the appointed date one must isolate oneself from all activity and even as far as possible change one's appearance and residence.

46. In no way should one register one's identity card during the meeting, as this declaration made after residence registration serves as fully convincing evidence. One must also, as far as possible, arrange that departure from home remains unnoticed.

47. When visiting many places, after each visit of a new town one must check whether anybody has followed him. At the slightest suspicion, one must take rigourous steps to lose the "tail."

48. If one brings literature, copying or duplicating equipment, etc. in his luggage, one must firstly see that the suitcase is not conspicuous by its weight. A large volume that is comparatively light is, therefore, better than a small but heavy package. In such cases one should not carry things from the carriage oneself, but look for a porter.

Various

49. One hiding from the spies in another town should remember that, however far this town might be from his former residence, there is no guarantee that he will not be recognised. Therefore, one ought not to appear in public places, the theatre or at the station, avoid crowded streets and try not to come out in the daylight.

50. One living illegally should often change his identity card or passport.

51. When registering a false identity card, keep one's flat completely clean and do not allow anyone to visit it .

52. A search or arrest on the basis of having been followed by spies stands in a different time relation to the latter, dependent on police considerations. Sometimes shadowing continues a very long time, over years, and then ends in a mass raid. At other time search or arrest is carried out on that same day or night when a given flat or individual has awoken the spies' suspicions. The changeability of this tactic must always be borne in mind. As soon as the fact of being followed is established, one must immediately take measures: either hide or destroy evidence and cease all relations with the organisation.

53. If someone has begun and then ceased to be shadowed, one can be sure that in future when an arrest is made those old secret notes will be produced; and if for some reason it would not be found necessary to show them, they will be attached to the file anyway.

54. In interrogations on should not admit anything about oneself or others or pay attention to threats. Nor should statements about others be believed even if they present signed protocols. Bear in mind that evidence of spies is often extremely false as a consequence of their often taking one individual for another, mistaking houses, floors, flats etc.

55. One should neither give nor take photographs from anyone, nor make inscriptions on them or keep photograph albums.

56. One should not keep books with initials or names of their owners.

57. The supplies for copying or duplicating equipment should not be bought in one place.

58. One should never send parcels, money, telegrams or registered letters to addresses which are given for ordinary letters.

59. Sending telegrams or faxes, one should remember their text is not destroyed. This should be borne in mind as regards both the content and handwriting.

60. One should not make notes in one's own handwriting on the margins of illegal books and newspapers.

61. Letters, documents etc. should preferably be destroyed by burning, trying not to leave ash.

GLORIOUS PAGES FROM THE POST-WAR HISTORY OF KGB

Quotations from *The Gulag Archipelago* by Alexander Solzhenitsyn illustrated by the most famous living Russian painter Mikhail Shemyakin.

From the victims themselves you will learn that they administer a salt-water enema in the throat and then put one in the 'box' cell for 24 hours to suffer from thirst.

Yes, yes Abakumov himself, the minister for State Security, in no way shies from this manual work (a Suvorov on the front line!), he is not against sometimes taking the rubber truncheon in his hands. His deputy Ryumin beats people all the more eagerly. He does it in Sukhanovka in the "general's" investigation office. The office has imitation walnut panelling on the walls, silk curtains on the windows and doors, a large Persian carpet on the floor. A dirty strip of carpet covered with blood stains is stretched over the floor for the victim of the flogging in order not to spoil this beauty. No simple overseer but a colonel helps Ryumin at the floggings.

"— So — Ryumin says politely, smoothing a rubber truncheon about 4 centimetres in diameter— you passed the trial by insomnia with honour — (Alexander Dolzhin was able to hold out a month without sleep by cunning — he slept standing up) — Now let us try the club. People don't hold out above two or three sessions. Take down your trousers, lie on the carpet." The colonel sits on the victim's spine. A.D. prepares to count the blows. He still does not know what exactly a blow with a rubber truncheon on the sciatic nerve means if the buttock has fallen away from long starvation. It is felt not where the blow falls — there is a splitting pain in the head. After the first blow the victim goes mad with pain, breaks his nails on the carpeting. Ryumin beats trying to make the blows fall accurately. The colonel presses with his body —just the job for three big stars on the epaulette to assist the all powerful Ryumin! (After a session the flogged man cannot walk and they do not carry him, they drag him along the floor, of course. The buttock quickly swells up so that it is impossible to button up one's trousers but there were practically no scars. Chronic diarrhoea breaks out and sitting on the pot in Solitary Dolzhin laughs. He must still endure a second session and a third, the skin will break. Ryumin, getting furious will have to beat him on the

gush out in an enormous hernia, they will take the prisoner to Butyrka prison hospital with peritonitis and the attempts to make him commit meanness will be temporarily suspended.)

But the most dreadful thing they can do to you is this: to undress you below the waist, to put you on your back on the floor, separate your legs. Assistants sit upon them (the glorious contingent of sergeants) holding you by he arms, and the investigator — even women are not too fastidious — stand between your separated legs and with the toe of their shoe (their slipper) gradually, by degrees and continually increasing the pressure, squeezing to the floor what made you once a man, look into your eyes and keep repeating their questions or propositions of treachery. If he does not press a bit harder prematurely you will have still fifteen seconds to cry out that you confess everything, that you are ready to imprison too those twenty persons they demand from you or slander in print anything you hold sacred.

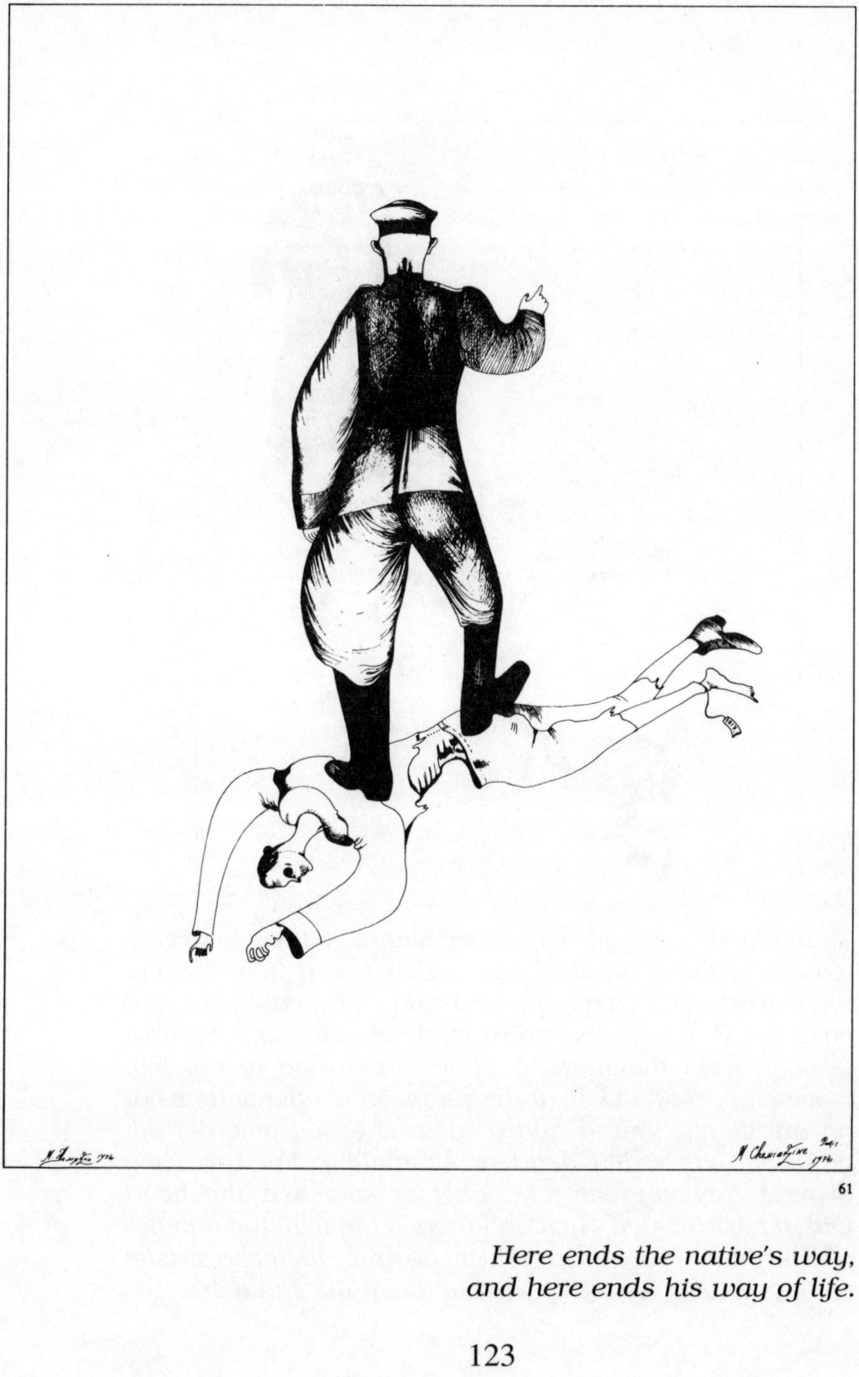

61

Here ends the native's way,
and here ends his way of life.

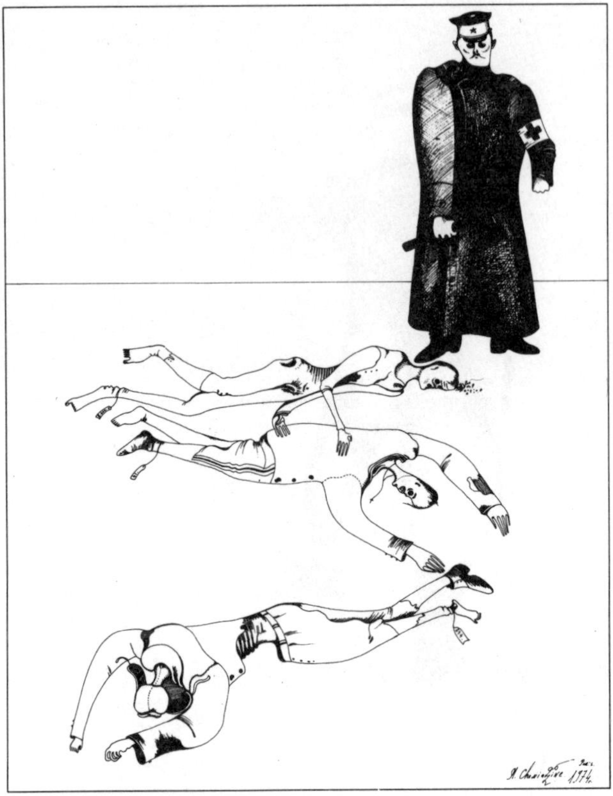

The cadavers shrivelled up from pellagra (without buttocks, women without breasts) and rotted away from scurvy, were examined in a morgue housed in a log-cabin or in the open air. Rarely it resembled medical autopsy: a vertical incision from the neck to pubis, fracturing of the leg, moving apart of a skull at the seam. More often it was not an antatomist but a guard who checked whether the prisoner was really dead or simulating. For this they pierced the body with a bayonet or smashed the head with a big hammer. Then and there a tag with the number of his prison file under which he was listed in prison records was attached to the big toe of the cadaver .

The corpses were removed on sledges or carts, depending on the season. Sometimes for convenience the put a box under six corpses; and when there was not a box, the hands and feet were tied together with a twine so they would not dangle. After this they would be dragged on top as logs and then covered with bast matting.

CONTENTS

Back cover photo:
Following the coup of 19th August 1991 Muscovites dismantle the monument to "Iron Felix" Dzerzhinsky on Dzerzhinsky Square in front of KGB headquarters.